MEN

ANDY WOLVERTON

DON'T

READ

THE UNLIKELY STORY
OF THE GUYS BOOK CLUB

CONTENTS

FOREWORD

To some, the sight of 14 men gathered around a table in a conference room would scream "business meeting." But the August 19 gathering of the Guys Book Club at the Severna Park Community Library was strictly for pleasure. Devoted readers, the men met to discuss *The Generals: American Military Command from World War II to Today* by Thomas E. Ricks. The mood was lighthearted as the meeting began. But when facilitator Andy Wolverton, a Severna Park branch librarian, asked for the guys' impressions of the book, the discussion took on a serious tone. One member described the book as "pretty bleak overall" while another said it revealed how badly wars were fought after World War II. A third thought the book was a good follow-on to July's book selection *The Guns of August*. Asked by Wolverton how they felt about the author's premise — if today's generals could be relieved for bad or poor performance, victory would be more attainable — most agreed. However, a vigorous conversation ensued about how to define "victory" and how that definition changes from conflict to conflict . . .

—Sharon Lee Tegler in *The Capital*, August 28, 2014

I first met Andy in 2016 when I attended my first meeting of the Guys Book Club. I'd read about the club in the summer issue of a local Severna Park newspaper, and after thinking about it for a few days, called the library for more information. The librarian who answered invited me to show up to discuss *Midnight in the Garden of Good and Evil* at the next meeting, on the third Thursday of August.

I'd never read the book and had never been involved with a book club, but I downloaded a copy to my Kindle and finished reading it two days before the meeting. Andy greeted me at the door to the library's conference room with a handshake and a big smile, found an unused name tent on the entry table (one of several that said "Steve"—a popular name in my birth era), and introduced me around the conference table. By the end of the meeting, I'd become an admirer of the book and a fan of the club.

Since you're reading this foreword, there's a good chance you already know that book clubs made up entirely of men are uncommon today. Groups such as Junto, Benjamin Franklin's 12-member literary society in Philadelphia, may have begun in the 18th century with all-male membership; but by the second decade of the 21st century, the overwhelming majority of the estimated 5,000,000 book club members in America are women. According to a 2018 survey of 5,000 U.S. book club members by the online magazine *BookBrowse*, the membership of nearly 90 percent of private book clubs are exclusively women while fewer than half of public book clubs (*e.g.*, those hosted by libraries) include a sprinkling of men. There are reasons for this, but none that decide destiny.

The first may be rooted in initial ability with a dash of preference on the side. Thanks to the industrial revolution and the widespread public education that fueled it, reading, writing, and mathematics became indispensable foundations of achievement around the globe. Universally, though, girls score higher as a group than boys do on tests of reading ability. According to the *2015 Brown Center Report on American Education*, boys' reading achievement lags behind that of girls in every country in the world. This gap has occurred at ages ranging from 9 through 15 since at least the 1940s, when the first large-scale survey was made. Predictably, part of the difference correlates with enjoyment—that is, most girls simply like reading more than most boys do. Yet in an international assessment of adults conducted in 2012, reading scores for men and women were indistinguishable from each other at ages up to 35; and by 55 and beyond, men had significantly higher scores than women. A different picture emerges, however, when the focus shifts to reading books. Nearly 60 percent of avid book readers in the youngest group (under 25) were women. By age 55, women made up an even larger share of devoted readers, while two-thirds of all respondents who said they never read books were men. In short, women remained more enthusiastic readers even as their scores in comprehension tests lagged men's scores.

Second, some of the conventional social characteristics of gender, at least in the west, may be in play here as well. Women famously value empathy, warmth, creativity, expressiveness, and sensitivity. Men are typically labeled vigilant, independent, rule-conscious, logical, and assertive. Women are encouraged to prefer socialization. Men notably seek dominance. And while all these traits are present to some degree in most women and most men, it's also undeniable that women as a group embody feminine attributes more often and to a greater extent than men do, and vice-versa. Moreover, gender roles not only promote increased expression of their relative components but inflict restrictions as well. (*He throws like a girl. She interrupts like a boy.*) Book clubs, I believe, provide a means for people to distance themselves from some of these restrictions for an hour or two each month. It seems perfectly natural then, when viewed from these layered perspectives, that there are not only a lot of men in the world who genuinely enjoy reading; but who also find the notion of discussing their ideas and reflecting on others' ideas about books and their connection to life genuinely compelling. *That's* the Guys Book Club of Severna Park that I've come to know.

The book at hand—Andy's book—identifies and explores the vision, engagement, patience, attention to detail, and persistence that gave birth to the Guys Book Club, as well as the blend of democracy and decisiveness that sustains it today as it nears its tenth year. Andy Wolverton is a genuinely extraordinary person, but the engaging, straightforward narrative he's written describes pieces and a process usable by anyone who wants to create a stimulating environment for men ready to read, share, and reflect on books in the company of each other. Such men are clearly not a majority, but a cursory analysis of the numbers above nonetheless suggests there are thousands on thousands of them.

This is Andy's story. If you read it carefully and with purpose, it can become your story too.

Steve Collier
Member, Guys Book Club of Severna Park

INTRODUCTION

"Men don't read." That was a phrase I heard often when I first became a librarian. I didn't believe it then and I don't believe it now.

I work at the Severna Park Library, one of 16 branches of the Anne Arundel County Public Library system based in Annapolis, Maryland. The Severna Park Branch is considered a medium-sized library in the AACPL system, serving a well-educated, upper-middle-class community of nearly 38,000.[1] Severna Park prides itself on excellent schools, a mixture of chain stores and independent merchants, and reasonably easy access to Annapolis and Baltimore (and if the traffic isn't too bad, Washington, D.C.). Centrally located within Anne Arundel County, the Severna Park Library serves a large group of patrons[2], many of whom are dedicated readers of all kinds of books, periodicals, and digital literature.

Our branch gets a tremendous amount of traffic, and although it's not the largest in the system, we frequently have the highest number of circulated items each month, which translates into a large number of readers. Many of those readers know which new titles are

---

1 U.S. Census Bureau, 2010, https://www.census.gov/quickfacts/table/PST045214/2471200/embed/accessible

2 As an AACPL library employee, I am expected to refer to library users as "customers," which I do when anyone official is within earshot, but prefer the term "patron." "Customer" seems to imply a monetary exchange, and unless you're paying a fine or purchasing something from the book sale area, the term strikes me as inaccurate.

coming out before we do. It's not unusual for people to come up to the Information Desk and request several titles to be placed on hold well before their release dates (and often before we even have records for those titles). I'm always glad to help people place these holds, not only because it's part of my job, but also because I like to get to know people and learn which books catch their interest. After a few of these encounters, I also enjoy learning what they like about the books they read, the choices they make, and how receptive they are to book suggestions. I always hope learning more about the patrons I serve will lead to ideas for other books I can recommend to them. (In the library world we call this readers' advisory, a skill we constantly seek to develop and refine to help readers of all ages and types.)

I'd estimate that 80% of the people who came to the Information Desk to place holds in the early days of my job were women. After I'd helped them several times over a period of weeks or months, I felt confident enough to ask, "What's your husband reading?" Okay, I know this was totally inappropriate and a terrible assumption on my part, but when I saw wedding rings on fingers and pictures of children and grandchildren as these patrons began digging through purses and wallets for their library cards, I felt it was a risk worth taking. As far as I know, no one was ever offended.

The answer I frequently received was, "Oh, men don't read."

Uh, hello? I'm a man standing right in front of you and I read, and other such thoughts ran through my mind. Only what I actually said was, "Well, *I* read."

"But you're a librarian," they'd usually say. "My husband doesn't read anything but the sports section of the newspaper."

Okay, maybe *that* woman's husband didn't read, but her husband wasn't *all* men. I'm not exactly qualified to write a textbook on logical reasoning, but just because one man doesn't read doesn't mean that all men don't.

Now I understand that woman was simply making a generalization, but I was still offended. She was wrong. Men *do* read, certainly not all men (or all women), but *some* men. In fact, I felt confident in my ability to prove it. I could recall (and name them, if necessary) at least half a dozen men who would regularly come up to the Information Desk with their reading lists and ask for books to be placed on hold *for themselves,* not for their wives. I also saw at least as many men come into the library on a regular basis, browse the new fiction and nonfiction books, go into the stacks for an extended period of time, and come to the checkout desk with at least a couple of books. Sure, those guys could've been picking up books for someone else, but I doubted it. I knew men were reading, maybe not *all* men, maybe not even all the men in Severna Park, but enough to possibly form a halfway decent book club for men.

I never wanted to hear the words "Men don't read" again in my library. So I did something about it.

CHAPTER 1

Getting Started

Let's be honest: most people of a certain age are not that interested in trying new things. That phrase "of a certain age" is important. Kids try new things all the time. The younger they are, the more they do so, mainly because they're picking up new life experiences at a very fast rate. As they grow older, a certain percentage of children will try anything new while others seem content within a small range of preferred activities. This willingness to try just about anything carries on into the teenage years with a recklessness sometimes resulting in utter embarrassment. ("Hey Jim, remember the time you tried to drink a dozen milkshakes?") Although the risk of trying new things often diminishes with age, many of us still avoid unknown ventures, even those that are relatively safe, such as a book club.

What in the world could be scary about a book club? You're in a room (hopefully somewhat comfortable), sitting down, probably with some type of refreshments, with no one placing you in a headlock or breaking out the thumbscrews. By and large, book clubs provide a safe atmosphere.

Yet some people don't want any part of it. Even some people *who love reading* don't want any part of it. I understand that. They read for their own pleasure, enlightenment, education, edification, or other reasons we could name, but they don't *really* want to share their thoughts with other people. Again, I understand that.

I also understand that people are busy. They're busy in the same ways people everywhere are busy: They have jobs, families, kids, homes to care for, responsibilities, commitments, hobbies, you name it. Time is valuable and when you have some to spare, you want to spend it doing things you *know* you enjoy. Trying something new and/or different is a bit like gambling. Will this activity be worthwhile, or will it suck time away from me, time I can't get back?

Add to these factors another important one: I live in the vicinity of two major cities, Baltimore, Maryland and Washington D.C. Many of the people in our library's service area commute to one or the other of these cities every day. These are not breezy, fun-filled commutes that make you want to roll down your car window, let the wind blow through your hair (if you have any), take a deep breath, and exclaim with delight, "Ah, life!" No, things move fast around here (except for traffic), people are in a hurry, they're often rude, grumpy, irritable, frustrated, frazzled, stressed out, exasperated, aggressive, mad, and just plain fed up with things in general. This happens, of course, in almost every city in the United States, but consider that we are scant miles away from our nation's capital, a cauldron of contention, disappointment, disagreement, and generally bad tempers regardless of who's in office.

When most people get home, they just want to chill.

I get that. All of this to say that I understood full well that starting a book club - and a book club for *guys* - was going to be an uphill climb.

And it was. The first few months of the Guys Book Club certainly weren't easy. It took a long time to develop a core audience. Who am I kidding? It took a long time to develop *any* audience. I had no idea if a book club for grown men was going to work. Guys themselves will admit that they're generally not "joiners." Even if they were, the truth of starting a new library program is this: Many new programs simply do not succeed, regardless of months of planning, research, and hard work. The reasons are legion. As I mentioned before, people are busy, their after-work time is limited, they have families, you picked the wrong night, etc. I know many librarians who plan ongoing adult-based programs and spend extraordinary amounts of time and resources only to have few or no people show up. (I have prepared at least two library programs in which *no one* showed up.) Library-based book clubs can be even more problematic, especially in an area like Severna Park where several independent book clubs already operate.

But we (my branch manager, my supervisor, and I) plowed ahead, and eventually the Guys Book Club *did* experience a level of success (otherwise I wouldn't be writing this book and you wouldn't be reading it), and it began to develop a consistent, dedicated audience. It wasn't long before other librarians began to ask me how I was able to get 10 or more (and sometimes more than 20) adult guys to come to the library each month to talk about books. I told them the truth: I spoke to every guy that came into the library.

"Yeah," these librarians would say, "but what did you do? Posters? Displays? Emails? What was your marketing strategy? Did you do in-branch surveys, send out questionnaires?"

"You don't understand," I'd reply. "I talked to *every guy* that came into the library. Every. Single. Guy."

And I did. I still get that question from other librarians who want to start a book club (not necessarily a guys book club) and I always answer it the same way. But when I do, they're usually disappointed, as if they were expecting - or hoping for - another answer. There *is* no other answer. You have to engage people on a personal level. There's no getting around it.

Maybe there *are* other ways for getting people to show up to programs: marketing strategies, surveys, the promise of prizes, food and drink, cruise tickets, sparkling diamonds, stock options, a weekend trip for two to the Outer Banks, whatever. What worked for me - and continues to work - is talking to individuals one at a time. That seems to frighten some of my fellow librarians, which is something I don't understand. Librarians talk to patrons every day; it's not like this is uncharted territory or learning a new language. It's what we do. We converse with people. It's not that hard. You say something, they say something. You say something back, they say something back. Repeat. Quantum physics and string theory are not (necessarily) involved. The keys to making it work are sincerity and a willingness to listen.

So it really wasn't that difficult to talk to the guys who came up to the Info Desk since I knew that most of those men were already interested in reading, at least on some level. But I also went up to men that *didn't* come up to the desk, guys who were content to be lone wolves, roaming around the stacks looking for an interesting read. You can often tell which ones are purposeful readers, looking for books according to a plan (often written on paper) and which ones are flying by the seat of their pants. Approaching the latter group of guys was tougher. I might start out with, "Hi. Can I help you find something today?" No matter how they answered, whether they said, "No thanks, I'm just looking" or "I'm just waiting for my wife" or "I just came in to cool off," I'd say, "We're starting a book club for guys. We'd love to have you join us. What types of books do you like?"

Their reactions were mixed. Some of these men were taken aback. Some stared in disbelief. Some backed away in sheer horror. But surprisingly, most were intrigued. "A book club? For *guys*?" was a popular response. (More than one person asked in all seriousness if there would be beer or liquor available. Sorry, no...) The guys who *were* interested listened to my pitch, nodding here and there, then said, "Thanks, I'll think about it," or something to that effect. A few were open and honest, saying that they loved reading but weren't comfortable discussing what they'd read with others. "I'm not really a joiner" is a response I'd hear from time to time. Regardless of their responses to my invitation, I'd thank them for listening and told them they were welcome to join us if they changed their minds.

But before any of those conversations happened, I had to plan out what the Guys Book Club was going to be. Clearly the readers were there in the community: I saw guys checking out books. I felt strongly that this library program was needed, and I knew that before convincing a bunch of guys that it was a good idea, I had to convince two people in my building: my supervisor and my branch manager.

At this point I'd been working at the Severna Park Library for two years. I learned early on in my career that the library is governed by a chain of command, much like the military (although the stakes are far different in our case). I first had to run my idea past my supervisor at the time, Heather, who would then run it by her supervisor, our branch manager, Karen.

I met with Heather and told her about my idea, telling her that I believed we had the readers if I could just convince them to come to the book club. She was receptive and asked me several questions about what I wanted the book club to look like, how it would function, etc. She mentioned that she was aware of a similar book club at the Miller Branch of the nearby Howard County Public Library system. She didn't know if it was still active but encouraged me to contact the organizer of that group to schedule a visit. I told her I'd check it out soon.

While we were discussing details, Heather asked me how often I wanted the group to meet. I told her that initially I'd like to meet every other month and see what developed, which she thought was a good idea, but offered a suggestion: since September is typically a busy back-to-school month, she suggested that I start the club in October. If I began in October and held meetings every other month, that would land our second meeting in December, typically a graveyard month for adult library programs. Heather recommended I hold two meetings during consecutive months in order to build momentum, skip December, then go bimonthly starting in January of 2012. I thought that was a good idea and agreed to it. That also meant that I would have to have my October and November books chosen before the *Happenings* (the library system's quarterly print schedule of programs and events) deadline in mid-June.

With those plans in place, I was ready to start making things happen. Then Heather asked me if I planned on serving refreshments. I guess I'd never realized that refreshments were an option. I asked Heather what I could serve, or rather what we could *afford* to serve.

"Not much," she said.

"How much is not much?" I asked.

"Not much at all," she said. So I decided to serve bottled water and microwave popcorn, both of which I could pick up in bulk and keep at the branch. I could also be reimbursed for both. The relatively low cost of these items would come out of the branch's overall programming budget (which was then, and still is, $250 a year).

As far as selecting books for the group, I told Heather that I had a pretty good idea for getting started, based on the guys I spoke to at the Info Desk on a regular basis, what would work and what wouldn't. I planned to stick mostly to nonfiction, mainly popular titles that would appeal to the guys I knew in our area: works of history, biography, sports, current events, etc. Heather cautioned me to make sure that the library system had enough copies of whatever I picked. "You don't know how large the group might get," she said, "so make sure there are at least 10 or more copies in the system."

Then she asked me a question I wasn't prepared for:

"How are you going to handle it when a woman shows up and wants to join the Guys Book Club?" I noticed that she said "when" and not "if."

I stared at her for a moment. "It's a *guys* book club," I said, as if this should be perfectly obvious.

Heather shook her head. "If a woman comes in and wants to be a part of the group, you have to let her in."

"But it's a *guys* book club! That's the whole point, to get men interested in reading, to bring *guys* together. There's tons of book clubs around for women!"

"You have to let them in," she said, and walked away. Although Heather is probably just a tad over five feet tall and could fit into many of the packages I receive from Amazon, she is a force of nature.

15

You do not want to mess with her. Yet I respectfully told her that I did not agree with her statement.

This was not the last time this topic would come up...

* * *

After a bit of research, I discovered that Howard County's Miller Branch indeed hosted a book club for guys called Dudes on Books. The sponsor's contact information was included on the library's website, so I emailed him, telling him that I wanted to start such a club at my library and asked if I could visit the group. Eric, the group's sponsor, replied that I was welcome to visit their next meeting.

At that time, Dudes on Books was run by two male librarians, both of whom appeared to be in their mid- to late-20s. Besides them, there were four or five men in attendance, all of them older than me (in my mid-40s at the time). They had a good discussion of *Zeitoun* (2010), the Dave Eggers nonfiction work about one Syrian-American man's experiences surviving Hurricane Katrina and its aftermath in New Orleans.

Eric and the other librarian had a list of questions they had prepared and for the most part, those in attendance answered the questions, gave their opinions, and stayed on topic. The conversations were good and the participants expressed thoughtful opinions, which is exactly what I had in mind for the Guys Book Club. The evening went well, but I never really understood why they had two librarians running the meeting, unless they both just liked having it set up that way. It seemed to work for them, and that was the main thing. Afterward, Eric shared a little more information about the group, mostly minor details. I thanked him for allowing me to visit, and he wished me luck, telling me I was welcome to drop in anytime.

That meeting didn't really provide any revelations, but it did solidify several things in my mind. First, I realized that I wanted to provide every guy in our group the opportunity to speak if he so desired. I didn't want the guys to feel like they were in a classroom where you were called on to give the "right" answer, but rather wanted them to feel that their opinions would be heard objectively, regardless of the popularity of those opinions.

I also realized that no one was going to come to the book club to hear *me* talk, which is a good thing. Before I was a librarian, I was a public school teacher for thirteen years, plus two years as a graduate teaching assistant while I was pursuing a doctorate in music. Stepping into "teacher mode" is almost second nature, but I knew I would have to consciously keep most of my teacher tools in the toolbox. This was not the place for them. While the organizational skills I'd learned and developed over the years would no doubt come in handy, I wanted to be more of a facilitator than an instructor.

It felt important to refrain from giving my personal opinions on a book unless one of the guys asked me to give it. While my stance on this modified slightly as time went on, I offered few thoughts of my own during those early months. Facilitating, rather than teaching or pontificating, would give people the opportunity to say what they wanted to say. I knew there would be times (there were, and sometimes still are) when I would have to move the conversation in a certain direction or possibly even away from a path that would be either irrelevant or dangerous (both of which happen, but not as often as you might think).

What I *wasn't* sure how to do was to convey the idea that differing opinions should be heard with as much respect and objectivity as the more popular opinions. This hadn't really been a problem with what I'd observed at the Dudes on Books meeting, but the group did have one member who spoke up often and was very opinionated. I didn't want to have someone in the Guys Book Club who had an ax to grind, so from the very beginning I determined not to choose any books focusing on religion or current politics. (Yet it's next to impossible to read *any* work of history, which I knew would potentially be a popular topic, without looking at the politics - and possibly the religion - of that era.) Of course, there are other axes to grind, but I hoped that by eliminating most of the religious/political discussions, I'd be able to put out any small brush fires that might flare up.

I had envisioned the Guys Book Club meetings happening this way:

- A brief introduction of the book - not a summary, but maybe a few things about the author, when and/or why the book was written, etc.
- An "icebreaker" question about the book, followed by discussion
- Various questions (from me) to generate discussion, hopefully following a logical line of thought or the chronology of the book
- Final thoughts including questions such as "What in this book spoke to you?" or "Who would you recommend this book to?" or "Would you read other books by this author or on this topic?" or even "What do we do with this book?" (or more pointedly, what do we do with the knowledge/experience we gained from reading this book?)

My hope was that the group would be very conversational, sort of like the writers' groups I'd been a part of years earlier in which each person gets the opportunity to speak without fear of interruption, judgment, ridicule, or scorn. I wanted an atmosphere of mutual respect and courtesy. I wanted thoughtful, meaningful conversations. I wanted laughter. I wanted bonding. I think more than anything else I wanted the guys who came to the meetings to go home with something new to think about, perhaps a challenge to the way they thought about a topic or a story. I wanted them to look at the world differently, even if just for that one moment.

So I had a plan in place. I didn't know how good it was, but it was a plan. Now I had to pick the all-important first book.

CHAPTER 2

The First Book

That first meeting was crucial. The date was set: Tuesday, October 18, 2011. At first the goal was simply to get guys to come through the door to see what this crazy thing called the Guys Book Club was all about. Some would no doubt come simply out of curiosity, but I was hopeful that others would welcome the opportunity to read and discuss books, but not just *any* books. That first book needed to be approachable, discussable, and popular, something that would appeal to a broad range of guys, yet not a book that was too simple or shallow.

Many of our regular guy patrons loved books by John Grisham, Clive Cussler, Lee Child, and other best-selling authors. While I have nothing against those writers, I realized their works are primarily light reads with not an awful lot in them to discuss. They're fine for what they are: casual or what we often call "beach" reads. You read them and typically don't think a lot about them afterward. Really, what's there to discuss? "Man, Jack Reacher really kicked butt in *that* one!" or "This book isn't as good as his last one," or "That would make a great movie!" A few such comments go by and you've still got 58 minutes left to kill.

Many of the guys I initially approached about the book club asked if we would be reading books by some of those popular writers. My response was usually noncommittal: "You never know," or "You'll have to wait and see." I could've simply said "No, we won't be reading James Patterson books. We'll be reading and discussing things that have real substance."

Was that how I felt? Yes. Did I say that, or something like it? No. I didn't want to start out negative. Those books have a place and they serve a purpose. Heck, I enjoy those writers and their books, but I don't want a steady diet of them. Yet I understand that others do, and I don't judge them for that. There's simply not much to delve into with those books. But at the same time, I didn't want to limit my audience too much. *If I go with works of popular fiction*, I thought, *I might get large numbers, but what's the point?* Is that the type of book club I wanted? The challenge was to choose books that would encourage guys to think and discuss things of importance, but books that were also enjoyable. We probably weren't going to cover *great* literature every time we met, but I certainly wanted (as much as possible) to strike a balance between substance, interest, readability, and approachability. But I also wanted, especially for the first book, something recognizable and popular.

That first book needed to be one that wasn't just recognizable, but one you couldn't get away from, a title everyone was talking about. I didn't want something moderately popular, I wanted something *wildly* popular, a book you couldn't say "No" to, a title that would draw in even the most reluctant participant.

I had two books to choose for the upcoming Sept/Oct/Nov 2011 issue of *Happenings* for our October and November meetings. After much thought and research, I decided the very first book discussed by the Guys Book Club would be *Unbroken* by Laura Hillenbrand. The book had been released in November 2010 and was enormously popular, eventually spending over four years on the New York Times bestseller list including 14 weeks at #1.[3] (The book has become the fifth longest-running nonfiction bestseller in history.[4]) So after choosing a high-profile book *and* talking to every guy that came into the library, I was confident that first meeting would be a sure thing.

Any book (or movie, TV show, etc.) that's universally hailed as great, a must-read, or an "instant classic" always makes me suspicious, which is why I never read Hillenbrand's first book *Seabiscuit: An American Legend* when it hit the shelves in 1999. At the time of its release, I was working in a small independent bookstore and nearly every person walking through the doors wanted *Seabiscuit*, one after another, every single day. Then those who had read it came back, wanting to buy another copy to give to someone. *Seabiscuit* wasn't just popular, it was a phenomenon.

Unbroken, the story of World War II POW Louis Zamperini, was on target to become even more popular than *Seabiscuit*. In spite of the hype, I read *Unbroken*, since World War II tales have always interested me much more than horse stories. *Unbroken* both impressed and moved me. I had no reservations in choosing it for the book club.

Soon the announcement of the Guys Book Club appeared in *Happenings* with information about our first two meetings. We would discuss *Unbroken* in October, and another book in November,

---

3   Laura Hillenbrand, "Laura Hillenbrand Unbroken: About the Book," 2010, accessed April 5, 2018. http://laurahillenbrandbooks.com

4   Ibid.

which I'll tell you about in the next chapter. Of course I didn't wait until *Happenings* came out to start talking to people about the book club. I continued my usual practice of talking to every guy who came into the branch. But now I had a title to share with them.

Once I began mentioning *Unbroken*, people started paying attention. Here was a book they'd heard of (How could you *not* have heard of it?), a book they'd read or wanted to read. While most of the guys I approached were familiar with the title, some didn't know what the book was about. When I described the story, they grew more interested. Many asked if we had the book, checking it out if we did and putting it on hold if we didn't. Copies were checking out, but I knew that wasn't necessarily an indicator of how many guys might show up, since many people in the general population were still reading the book as well. I felt encouragement mixed with a bit of queasiness.

The night of the first meeting I set up a table and several chairs in the library's meeting room (which holds well over 150 people) and waited. Signs on the meeting room door announced that this was the place for the book club. The refreshments didn't exactly constitute a banquet fit for kings, but at least microwave popcorn and bottled water were both within my meager budget. So 7pm rolled around, and….

Three guys showed up.

I kept telling myself, "Hey, three guys isn't bad." It could've been worse. We've had adult library programs before where *nobody* showed up. And while I was thankful *anyone* had come, I'll admit feeling a little disappointed. But I had to hide that disappointment and give it my best for the three guys who were there.

One of them was a regular library patron who often came up the Info Desk to place books on hold. I'll call him Daniel. Daniel was probably in his late 70s, a guy in good shape who looked like he might've been an athlete as a young man. I always enjoyed talking with Daniel at the desk; he was a very personable guy and always enjoyed talking about books, vacationing and fishing. From the first moment I mentioned the Guys Book Club, Daniel was on board, although most of what he read consisted of popular books by authors like David Baldacci, John Grisham, and Clive Cussler. Daniel also read popular nonfiction, so I felt he would probably enjoy *Unbroken*. Watching Daniel walk through the door for that first meeting immediately put me at ease.

Paul was a gentleman I had seen in the library on several occasions, but had never spoken to, a tall man, probably in his mid-60s, someone who seemed very personable. The third gentleman was someone I'd never seen in the library before. I'll call him Robert, a man I guessed was in his mid-70s. Robert was also tall, the kind of guy who looks as if life hasn't really dealt him a bad hand, but he likes to give the impression that it has, with lots of sighing, long exhalations, and never looking you in the eye. I felt good about Daniel and Paul. I wasn't so sure about Robert.

What I *was* sure about was that my marketing technique of talking to every guy in the library had been a complete bust. Here we were at the first meeting, and two-thirds of the guys in attendance had never been approached by me. Even worse, all those conversations I *had* conducted with other guys in the library had proven a wasted effort. But it was too late to do anything about it at that moment, so I pressed ahead with the three guys who were there.

To be honest, I was very thankful I had three guys. It could've been zero. One of the problems with trying new programs at the library without preregistration is that you never know how many (or more accurately, how few) people you'll get at your program. Of course, preregistration doesn't guarantee those people will show up, but at least you have an idea about the level of interest. As I mentioned before, I've planned other programs where *no one* showed up, so I really had no reason to complain about that night's turnout.

So the four of us gathered around a single table. I sat on one long side of the table with Daniel at my right. Across from Daniel sat Paul, and Robert placed himself at the "head" of the table (to Daniel's right and Paul's left). I didn't think about it at the time, but later I began wondering about the personalities of people based on where they sit at meetings. It seemed Robert's choice of seating equated to something of a "power" position, and although I'd never met him before, I wondered if he might try to dominate the meeting.

I thanked everyone for coming and asked how they found out about the group.

"You told me about it," Daniel said, tossing popcorn into his mouth, chewing and grinning like he was part of an exclusive secret club. Paul had seen one of my signs posted in the library about the book club, and Robert had noticed the announcement in *Happenings*. As an icebreaker (and with plenty of time, having only three participants), I asked each guy to tell a little about themselves, which they gladly did. Daniel and Robert were both retired; Paul was not. As far as I could tell, none of these men had met before, although they all lived in either Severna Park or Arnold (the next town south of Severna Park).

To be honest, I don't remember much about the initial discussion of *Unbroken*. I had lots of notes on a legal pad as well as a copy of the book with several sections marked with Post-it notes, but I probably began with something like, "What struck you most about the book?" or "What aspects of the book really spoke to you?"

My mind was racing, trying to process too many things at once. I was ecstatic that my dream had become a reality. Here were actual living, breathing guys who had left the comfort of their homes to come to the public library to sit down and talk with other guys about a book we had all read. This was amazing! In a moment of hubris, I thought, "The newspaper should be here to cover this! GUYS *DO* READ!!! I HAVE PROOF!!!" Everything in me wanted to open the meeting room doors wide so that passersby could see this 21st century miracle taking place: Guys getting together to talk about books! *Come and see! Step right up, you won't see this anywhere else! Yes, ladies and gentlemen, this is not an illusion, there are no wires, no smoke and mirrors, just real guys reading real books and discussing them! Come and see!*

My mind raced to plans for the next meeting and how to increase attendance. *If I can get three guys to the first meeting, I'll bet I can get six at the next one. Maybe even ten!*

My daydreams lasted only a few moments. These guys were starting to open up and play off each other's comments, elaborating, giving personal anecdotes and experiences related to the book, basically keeping the conversation moving. Only a few times did I interject questions when I felt the momentum might be lagging, but the guys were really living up to my expectations.

Except for Daniel. He pretty much just sat there and ate popcorn.

Wanting to get him engaged in the conversation, I asked Daniel what he thought about the portion of the book that Paul, Robert and I were discussing. "I thought it was great," Daniel said. After a few other attempts to get Daniel more involved, I soon realized something that would turn out to be one of the earliest lessons I learned from the Guys Book Club: Every guy is different and not everyone is going to participate in the group in the same way at the same level of interest and intensity. I'll discuss this more as we go along, but at the time, this realization was a shot of reality.

Though overall the discussion was going well: no lags, no uncomfortable stretches of silence, just two of the three guys participating, expounding on my questions, and taking the discussion in interesting places without getting off topic. Then something happened that I just knew was going to wreck the meeting, if not the future of the Guys Book Club.

Robert began reflecting on the themes of racism touched on in *Unbroken*, how many Americans during World War II unjustly considered anyone of Asian heritage to be "the enemy," whether they were fighting on the side of the Axis or simply trying to provide a better life for their families as law-abiding American citizens. Robert continued (and I paraphrase): "I remember a time when you couldn't buy a house in Severna Park if you were Asian. I also remember a time when you couldn't buy a home here if you were black or Catholic."

Not knowing Robert, I wasn't exactly certain if he was finished. I felt as if he had more to say, but wasn't sure how much more. I also had some anxieties that the road he was traveling down might be one I couldn't steer us out of before the wheels fell off. I was about to find out.

(Again, I paraphrase.) "Sure," Robert continued, "there was a lot of discrimination going on in this area. And who knows what would've happened if two gay men tried to buy a house?"

Silence.

"My son is gay," Paul said.

There it is, I thought, the spark that ignited the explosion that ended the Guys Book Club in its first - and probably last - meeting. Paul had said it in a quiet, yet very distinct, articulated manner that could've been easily taken as either a simple statement or a challenge, and I didn't know him well enough to know which. For a couple of precarious seconds, the world was suspended in a volatile quiet that made me tense. That span of silence, while it seemed eternal, provided me scant seconds to think about all the different ways I could defuse the situation, calm tempers, soothe emotions, and have everyone escape from the meeting unscathed. I opened my mouth to speak, unsure of what I was about to say, but before I could utter a syllable, Robert turned to Paul and said, in a soft, calm voice, "How did you react when you found out?"

Paul folded his hands and let out a breath. "I told him I love him. What else would I do?"

Of all the things I expected to happen during those tension-filled seconds, empathy was not high on the list, yet that's exactly what happened. Paul went on to recount that his son's revelation to him was unexpected, yet he knew that the love he has for his son was not impacted in the least. His son is his son and always would be regardless of his sexual orientation.

Robert took all of this in, nodding his head slowly. You could tell that he probably had had little to no experience in such confrontations, yet clearly he was processing this moment in a way that I

29

hoped was positive. This was, as one of my favorite writers Flannery O'Connor calls it, a moment of grace, a situation in which her fictional characters (often through violence) come to see the world through a revelatory lens, changing their ways of thinking and possibly their lives. Here was an open, honest moment of sharing from one complete stranger to another, a sharing that was not ridiculed, criticized, or laughed away. It was respectful. When Robert asked Paul how he reacted, it was clear that Robert wasn't making a judgment; he really wanted to understand a situation he had probably never been faced with before. This was it, exactly what I'd hoped for: two guys being totally honest with each other, opening themselves up, and being vulnerable in the presence of other guys.

Once I realized a fight wasn't going to break out, I was stunned. In telling my branch manager about this exchange, I found myself overcome with emotion. I wanted the Guys Book Club to bring people together, to share their lives through books, but I'd never counted on anything this powerful and honest. When you ask people to share something together, whether it's a book, a movie, or any other experience, you invite the possibility of diverse opinions and varying reactions to those experiences. What you hope for is a situation in which people listen to and think about different types of thoughts without attacking them, seeking first to understand a concept from someone else's point of view.

This isn't just using a book club selection as a jumping-off point leading to a slightly (or wildly) different discussion. Yes, it's entirely possible that we will briefly use a book or a section of a book as a springboard into some other topic. But it's always essential to *start* with the book and eventually bring the discussion *back* to the book. But you certainly can't ignore such moments of grace.

Incidents like the one described above can be powerful, unforgettable events that cause people to reflect in a meaningful way on what was just discussed, but they can also make other members uncomfortable, not necessarily because of the subject matter being discussed, but because of the potential level of intimacy they invite. This is not to say that guys are unwilling to talk openly about their feelings. Many are; others are not. Part of my job as the facilitator of the group is to quickly evaluate where these personal (sometimes *highly* personal) stories are going, how they might benefit the group, and how long to let them go. After leading a few book club discussions, you start to pick up on who's comfortable with such transparency and who's not. I try to look for body language. Folded arms, scowls, eyes looking down at the table, etc., are often indicators that participants are not engaged or are uncomfortable and ready to move on. Yet you don't want to discount someone else's experience and move on too quickly.

These are all somewhat spur-of-the-moment decisions that facilitators are often required to make. The subject matter of some books can lend itself to personal stories of various degrees. Don't be surprised if a business book like *Good to Great* by Jim Collins leads to a soul-bearing episode, and a book potentially loaded with personal stories such as Harper Lee's *To Kill a Mockingbird* does not. You just never know. You must be prepared for just about anything. I learned that lesson during our first meeting and have never forgotten it.

What kind of reaction would my second book choice provoke? A group hug? Fisticuffs? Our next meeting was a month away. As indicated earlier, I had already chosen the November book, another nonfiction work, but one wildly different from *Unbroken*. I'd only gotten three guys to show up after picking an enormously popular book. What would I get when choosing something completely different?

CHAPTER 3

The Second Book

In many ways that first meeting made the rest of my marketing efforts much easier. Now all I had to do was go up to any guy in the library (other than the three who'd attended the first meeting) and say, "We missed you at the last Guys Book Club meeting. It was fantastic! Hey, we're going to have another one soon," at which point I would hand them a copy of *Happenings* turned to the page with our Guys Book Club information. "I hope to see you there!"

My approach made three things clear to them:

(1) By saying "*We* missed you at the last meeting," I implied that somebody besides me had attended. These guys I spoke to didn't know if two or 25 people had showed up, but *someone* had, and it hadn't been a complete bust.

(2) Another gathering was planned. Whatever happened, that initial meeting must have been good enough to justify a second one. I could imagine them thinking, "If it had been a total train wreck, they wouldn't let them do it again." The powers that be were going to allow this crazy librarian to continue this madness.

(3) I was asking *them* to attend the next one. In their minds this was an event that, despite the odds, had happened and

was going to happen again, which meant this librarian guy wasn't a complete yoyo, and he wasn't going to give up so easily. In effect this was a *personal* invitation to meet with other guys who might just like the same things they like. Hopefully they would see that my interest wasn't *just* in building numbers, but also in offering them an opportunity to be around like-minded guys. You like reading books? So do these guys. Do you like a good discussion? We do too. Let's get together.

So I kept talking to people. I talked to wives. I handed out lots of copies of *Happenings* with the Guys Book Club section highlighted. Fortunately I had lots of time to do this since our next meeting was a month away.

The November book was difficult to pick. In fact, picking books months in advance is always tricky. Since library book clubs must choose their titles months in advance to get them in *Happenings*, I don't have the luxury of choosing a book, discussing it, evaluating the group's response to it, then picking the next book based on their reaction.

It would be safe to continue to pick another nonfiction title, but for our second book, I wanted something a little off the beaten path. I decided on a book that wasn't as familiar or popular as *Unbroken*. (What book *would've* been as familiar or popular?) After much thought, I chose *Born to Run: A Hidden Tribe, Superathletes, and the Greatest Race the World Has Never Seen* by Christopher McDougall, a book whose title implies that it is *not* going to be (1) a book about Bruce Springsteen, or (2) your typical, conventional nonfiction read.

McDougall is a long-distance runner who frequently suffers injuries and wanted to discover ways he could run longer with fewer setbacks. He heard about the Tarahumara Indians, who live in relative seclusion and secrecy in Mexico's Copper Canyons. The Tarahumara can run literally hundreds of miles with little to no rest or injuries, and McDougall was determined to discover their secrets. The book is a spellbinding read filled with strange characters, heart-pounding running, exotic locations, and one of the strangest, most surreal races ever documented. It contains some of the most amazing descriptions of what (supposedly) normal humans can achieve. An odd book, but hopefully an inspiring one.

Born to Run might be a hard sell, so I decided to do something I hadn't done the first time: reach its target audience of runners. I contacted several running clubs, inviting them to join us, thinking "What the heck, why not? Hey, I might as well also contact stores that specialize in running shoes and apparel." So I did.

I spoke to library patrons whom I knew (or even suspected) were runners. Most of them hadn't heard about the book and were intrigued.

At least that's what they told me. All our copies were soon checked out, so I felt encouraged.

At the meeting for *Born to Run*, two guys showed up: a man and his teenage son.

Two guys. Nobody from the running clubs I'd contacted, nobody from the athletic stores, none of the runners I'd spoken to in the library. Two guys.

Self-doubt was right there on my shoulder, but I tried not to allow it to overwhelm me. Even though only two guys had shown up, they were both enthusiastic about the book, so that was encouraging.

The son was a serious runner and he'd wanted his dad to come ever since he'd heard the group would be discussing *Born to Run*. We had a good discussion, and both father and son had a great time.

There were some positives that came out of that second meeting. First, a teenager had found out about it and dragged his dad along. I had managed to connect with someone who really wanted to read and discuss the book based on its subject matter. If I could reach two guys, I knew I could reach more.

Second, these guys seemed enthusiastic enough to come back to future meetings. (And they did. More on that in Chapter 6.) Yet while they were both enthusiastic about the book, and I was delighted to have a teenager join the group, I was disappointed that there wasn't a larger turnout.

I just didn't understand it. I'd spoken to more people, put more *Happenings* into more hands, had carried on more conversations with more guys, had even contacted running groups and athletic stores, and only two people had shown up. Where were all these guys I'd spoken to? Why were they staying away? Was it really because men aren't joiners? The readers were out there, I was convinced of it.

What hurt even more was something I didn't realize until several hours after that second meeting: not one of the three guys from the first meeting had shown up.

Maybe it was my approach. Was I coming on too strong? Could it be that I had chosen the wrong books, specifically the wrong *second* book? Everybody knew about *Unbroken*, but not many people I'd spoken to were aware of *Born to Run*. Perhaps it was too off-the-wall, too odd, too lacking in general appeal.

Or maybe it was the time of the year. It was November when people are making their Thanksgiving plans, which might include travel. This *was* the middle of November, after all, perhaps too close to the holiday. Maybe it was a combination of all these things, but it was discouraging.

I still felt my approach was a good one. One-on-one personal conversations, I believed, was the best way to get guys to come to meetings. Contacting people from running groups and athletic stores just didn't have the personal touch of the one-on-one conversations. Instead of calling and emailing them, I should've visited their locations and talked to people, sort of like an outreach visit. And although I wasn't seeing the immediate benefit, I was making more and more connections with a larger number of guys. Despite the low numbers, I was committed to that approach.

If the approach wasn't the problem, it had to be either me or the book.

I've never considered myself a pushy, high-pressure, used-car salesman type of guy. I'd never worked in sales, but in a way, I had. Teaching band to kids from sixth grade to high school for 13 years gives you some experience in "selling." When you're competing with other extracurricular or elective classes, you sell your program, not only to the kids, but also to their parents, since (in most cases) they'll be making a financial investment in an instrument. I had to convince them that their kids would have a lot of fun, learn how to read, play, and appreciate music, and would learn to work as a team. Part of that sales toolbox included selling them on the fact that music broadened their lives, developed their minds in fun and unique ways, and would help them in many other parts of their educational journey. I sincerely believe all of that, and sincerity helps. But mostly

I had to convince kids that they were going to have a great time with their friends. Maybe I *was* a salesman.

If so, I didn't feel I was a *pushy* salesman. As I mentioned earlier, I had developed a good rapport with several of the regular library patrons. I didn't think they'd consider me someone who would sell them a used car or refrigerators at the North Pole. I tried to "sell" guys on the idea that if you enjoy reading and having conversations about what you read, I'll provide a place where you can do that and have a good time doing it. So I hoped I wasn't the problem.

Maybe it was the books themselves. Perhaps I had made a huge mistake in not consistently asking people beforehand the types of books they would like to read. I could've simply put questionnaires out at the service desks and asked for feedback that way. (My co-worker Stephanie used this method a few years later and experienced great success with it.)

But would it have worked? These are *guys* we're talking about here, and most guys I know usually aren't all that jazzed about filling out questionnaires and surveys. Who knows how many I would've even gotten back? No, it was too late for a questionnaire or a survey. To do so at this point would've looked desperate (which I pretty much was).

Or, since I was so fond of talking to people in person, I could've just asked them what they wanted to read rather than shove my choices down their throats. I should've asked their opinions rather than trying to figure out their tastes on my own. These are the things you think of after the fact.

I felt that I could modify my approach somewhat, simply asking guys the types of books they'd like to read. But while keeping their opinions in the mix, I also wanted to give them something they weren't even aware they were looking for. Heck, if I could do that, I could probably give up library work and become a force to be reckoned with in actual sales or politics. (Okay, *forget* politics…) When you think about it, selling is exactly what librarians do every day when people are asking for a good book or movie. In fact, it's much easier than the "selling" I did as a band director. I just had to figure out my current market: guys.

But while trying to figure that out, I knew that for my third book, I would have to pick something amazing.

One thought came to mind, over and over, a thought that just wouldn't leave me. It was a statement from a veteran library programmer: "If your program hasn't produced numbers after two or three meetings, abandon it." Other people had told me "Know your community and give them what they want." While I agreed with both thoughts in theory, I knew that I really needed to give the book club more than two meetings. As for the other advice, I felt I *did* know my community. Those readers were out there. What I had to do was to convince them that I was giving them something they *did* want. The problem was that not enough of them *recognized* that was what they wanted.

How does change usually happen? Slowly. Sure, technology changes quite rapidly, and who are the people who generally adopt technological changes the quickest? The young. (Generally.) I felt that most of the guys I was targeting in the library were probably in their mid-40s and older. Those guys are typically slow to change. Sure, the formation of a book club for guys wasn't exactly earth-shattering news, but it *was* something new and different. I began to think that the "new and different" for the guys I was dealing with might take time. Maybe if I had enough staying power, good things would start to happen, and guys would start to catch on. Maybe.

At this point the book club was set to meet every other month, so since we were skipping December and February, I only had to choose one book for the next *Happenings* cycle (the December, January, February 2012 issue). I was also beginning to think the next book might be our *last* book. If the numbers weren't coming in after three meetings, I'd be expected to put the program out of its misery. I began wondering just how low the numbers had to get, and for how long, before I had to pull the plug on the Guys Book Club.

CHAPTER 4

The Third Book

With a little time to think about my third pick for the Guys Book Club, a little experience provided an advantage. Of the first two books, a wildly popular one had brought in three people and a more obscure one had brought in two. Maybe the second book was *too* obscure. The next book needed to be something more familiar, more approachable, more established.

We hadn't discussed any fiction up to that point, so maybe this would be a good time for a novel. But what kind? Something modern? A classic? A tough-guy book along the lines of Hemingway or something less literary? A lot of guys who come to our library read books by John Grisham, Clive Cussler, Vince Flynn, David Baldacci, Lee Child, etc. Maybe that was what would get guys to come to this third (and possibly last) meeting. Nothing against those authors, but those books were too narrow in scope.

I began scouring the Internet for lists of books for men, using Google for searches like "best books for men" or "novels for men" or other such terms. Previous searches had provided several good ideas, but this was the first time I realized how many classics appeared on those lists, books like *The Call of the Wild, Walden, The Art of War, Don Quixote, Robinson Crusoe,* and others. Would any of those titles work? They might yield good discussions, but only if the guys would actually *read* them.

Perusing these titles brought to mind the difficulty of getting high school students interested in reading the books on their required reading lists. We see this problem at the library all the time. Many of those students (and not just guys) come into the library with their assigned book lists and simply don't want to read anything from more than a decade ago, much less books published over a century ago. In many cases the arcane language is a turnoff, to say nothing of the length of some of those works. Would adult guys be any different?

The aisle of our library's Classics section gave me several ideas. Some writers and their works immediately leapt out: Poe, Hemingway, London, maybe Dickens… Poe might be too weird this early in the game. Dickens would probably be too long, with the exception of *A Christmas Carol*, which had the handicap of being everywhere, saturating the reading landscape so much and for so long that few adult men would seriously want to read it.

I went back through the section alphabetically. Richard Adams: no. Jane Austen: I'd love to pick an Austen novel, but now was not the time. Bronte: Same. Wouldn't it be great to pick *Jane Eyre*? But not now. Defoe? Perhaps *Robinson Crusoe*… Maybe. Dickens? No, for reasons previously mentioned. Dostoevsky? Sadly, no. Too Russian, too long. E.M. Forster? Too British. Thomas Hardy: no. Henry James: no. James Joyce: hell no.

Hemingway? Maybe, but which one? *The Old Man and the Sea* was too short. *For Whom the Bell Tolls* was too long. *The Sun Also Rises* was a possibility. I would've preferred a collection of

Hemingway stories, but I wasn't sure how to go about leading a discussion of a short story collection.

Jack London would probably be safer, but maybe these guys were forced to read London when they were kids. No matter what book I chose, there were probably guys who'd been forced to read it in school. One thing to avoid was bringing up memories of required reading lists and the negative connotations often associated with them. But with a classic, how could such situations be avoided?

Traveling up and down the Classics aisle, Hemingway came to mind again and again. Maybe he *was* the guy to go with. *The Sun Also Rises* was short enough, and, from what I remembered, filled with disillusionment and regret, perhaps not concepts to explore quite this early in the book club.

Then everything stopped. To the left of Hemingway, stood Dashiell Hammett's *The Maltese Falcon*.

For a moment I got very excited, thinking *This is it! This is the book!*

But wait. This was a book *I* wanted to read again and discuss. The 1941 John Huston film version of *The Maltese Falcon* starring Humphrey Bogart has been a personal favorite for decades, as has the book. But perhaps others wouldn't feel the same. Maybe the film (if they'd even seen it) was enough, and they didn't want to read the book. Just because I loved it didn't mean *they'd* love it. (This is always an important consideration when choosing books for your club.)

It was crucial to take myself out of the equation. Sure, there was the nostalgia factor that might work, but did the book stand on its own merits? *The Maltese Falcon* is a great story with great characters, but it also touches on some thought-provoking concepts: lies and deception, disillusionment, greed, the abandonment of principles, the clinging to principles, gender roles, desperation, manipulation… The list goes on and on. There was more than enough to discuss about the book *if* guys would show up to discuss it.

Plus, at just over 200 pages, the book was far shorter than our first two titles. Even if they didn't care for it, the novel wouldn't take very long to read. Another point in its favor.

Were there any downsides to choosing *The Maltese Falcon*? Anytime people read a book that's been adapted into a popular movie, the tendency for the reader is either to talk only about the movie or spend a large amount of time comparing the book to the movie rather than focusing on the book, which was why we were there in the first place. By choosing the Hammett novel, that was a possibility.

Again, this book was in the Classics section, so maybe some teenagers who had seen the book on their required lists might come to the meeting, possibly even with their dads who had seen (and hopefully enjoyed) the film at some point in their lives and wanted to try the book, a sort of father-and-son book club experience. And we certainly had plenty of copies.

The black bird was in. For good or for bad, *The Maltese Falcon* would be our third book, probably the best choice for attracting guys to the club. What did I have to lose?

For this third meeting, the group moved from its first location in the massive meeting room to the much smaller conference room, which consists of four long tables placed together to form one large rectangular surface. Twelve guys can sit around those tables comfortably, plus there was no need to tie up the Meeting Room, keeping out a community group or a homeowners association meeting whose numbers would certainly dwarf ours. The Conference

Room would provide a better atmosphere, a place where we would be out of sight. If this was to be our last meeting, out of sight might be a good place to be.

In the days leading up to the event, I continued talking to guys as they came into the library, promoting the book. "You've probably seen the movie," I'd tell them, and almost every time I'd get a nod. "Well then, you've just *gotta* read the book!" I described the novel's tough talk, the allure of the criminals, the betrayals, the danger. I extolled the mesmerizing story of the black bird, the colorful characters…. And I wasn't above ending my pitch with "It's the stuff dreams are made of…" (This line never appears in the book, only in the 1941 movie.)

At the Info Desk, I noticed a couple of guys checking the book out, so maybe at least one of them might show up. How many guys would it take to keep the book club going? Five? Six?

Daniel would come, and perhaps Paul would return as well. Plus the two aforementioned guys checking out the book, which is never a guarantee of attendance, but is a strong indicator. So at least four people seemed solid.

The next step was to improve the visual marketing. For the first two books, I'd created an advertisement on the library's upcoming programs board, an 8 1/2 x 11 poster that anyone would see when dropping off materials inside the branch. I placed more posters around the library, usually on the new book displays and in other high-profile spots. These posters were simply Word documents consisting of a large image of the book cover underneath the words "Guys Book Club" in a large font size. Below the photo I listed the date, time, and location. Simple and to the point.

Samantha Zline, a coworker, offered some valuable advice. Sam has a good eye for what works visually and what doesn't. She suggested a landscape format which placed the book cover on the left-hand side of the page, taking up half the 8 1/2 x 11 sheet of paper. Suggesting that Microsoft Publisher would be easier to work with than Word, Sam advocated for two boxes to the right of the photo: on top, a short blurb about the book (either from the publisher, a review, or a tagline) and on the bottom, the pertinent information of date, time, etc.

Sam's idea was an excellent one, but what I decided to do instead was think of something that might pull in guys who were unfamiliar with the book, but *were* familiar with other popular current writers. So my text read:

Before Harry Bosch, Jack Reacher, or Spenser, there was Sam Spade…

…followed by Guys Book Club, Tuesday, January 17, 2012, 7:00 pm, Severna Park Library.

With several Michael Connelly devotees out there, even more Lee Child readers, plus a healthy amount of Robert B. Parker fans, naming the protagonists of some of their series might be the connection the guys needed. Sure, it was a little misleading since Connelly's Harry Bosch is an LAPD police lieutenant working as a homicide detective in the Bosch series and not strictly a *private* detective, and Child's Jack Reacher is a former major in the U.S. Army Military Police Corps who's basically a drifter (although he solves a lot of crimes), and also not a detective. Only Robert B. Parker's Spenser (whose first name readers never officially learn) is a true private detective.

But none of that really mattered. It was only a way to establish a connection between the fictional characters these guys *did* know with Sam Spade, a character they probably *didn't* know. It's a technique we use in the library all the time in what we call readers' advisory: suggesting books you might like based on ones you've already enjoyed. (For instance, "If you like John Grisham's courtroom thrillers, try books by Greg Illes." Seriously, read Greg Illes.)

The poster wasn't too busy; it said just enough and more importantly, the book cover was eye-catching: the top half of the book was a painting of a stern-looking tough guy's face; below, an attractive woman with a serious but possibly deadly look in her eye. A blazing red banner with the title and author separated the two characters, a banner you couldn't help notice, which was exactly the right look.

The poster looked good, but Sam said that it wasn't eye-catching enough. She suggested a thin (but not too thin) border around the entire document, a red border, which made the banner from the book cover stand out. Satisfied, I posted these all over the library.

Finally the date came. I opened the door to the Conference Room at about 6:45pm and a couple of guys, both newcomers, immediately entered. Fifteen minutes early? This was good. As I introduced myself to them, another guy came in. Then another. Then two more. I wondered if some of them had come for a community association meeting and were in the wrong room. They weren't. They were all carrying copies of the book.

Soon most of the seats were taken, and guys were still coming in. By the time I'd welcomed everyone, I looked at the clock. It was 7pm on the nose, and I had 12 guys in the room ready to discuss the book.

Some of the guys were familiar. Others were strangers. They were all so immediately comfortable together I wondered if they all actually knew each other. Everyone was focused, attentive, and eager to talk. Sure, many of them talked about the movie and the differences between the two formats, but otherwise the discussion of the film itself was minimal. It quickly became clear that everyone had something to contribute, yet they were all willing to wait their turn before jumping into the conversation. Although I was prepared to do so, I didn't have to direct traffic. These guys were all respectful drivers. The thing was largely running itself, which allowed me to sit back and watch something spectacular unfold. Here was the evidence that guys *do* read. Not only do they read, they delight in talking about what they read.

Wow...

My excitement level was so high that I've forgotten much of what was said at the meeting, but I know we talked about the characters, their methods of deception, the code that Sam Spade refers to in "doing something" about the murder of his partner, the concept of the femme fatale, and much more. We discussed how Hammett portrays Spade with characteristics that make us think of Satan much more than the Humphrey Bogart performance implies. Images linger: guys attentively listening to whomever was speaking at the time, faces lighting up when someone articulated a thought or feeling they had also experienced, an acknowledgment of a shared idea, an opinion that matched or perhaps differed from their own.

No one changed the subject. No one checked his watch in boredom. No one looked at his cell phone. No one left early. They were not just having a discussion, they were *engaged* in discussion.

This was really happening!

I watched it all play out like a kid watching his favorite football team with a different player scoring a touchdown every time he touched the ball. But I wasn't the only person enjoying the discussion. They were all having a great time: people were smiling, laughing, listening to each other, acknowledging that they saw the same things as they were reading the book. This exceeded my wildest expectations.

There wasn't any one reason why guys finally showed up in larger numbers that night. A few said afterward that they'd been meaning to come previously, but had just never been able to make it until now. Others said that they'd loved the movie for years and wanted to read the book. At that point, I didn't care if they were there for the free popcorn. I was just overjoyed to have them there.

I hadn't really given much thought to how I'd manage a discussion with a large group. We'd never had one! With more participants, they sort of led themselves from one topic to another, sensing when they had explored a particular topic to its logical ending point before moving on to a new one. That is one of the aspects of the group that has continued to impress me, no matter how large or small attendance has been. Part of that comes from the fact that all these guys are respectful of each other, and that's not because they all share the same opinions; they don't. Yet they're willing to listen respectfully to differing viewpoints with an open mind. Very rarely have I had to step in and referee a potential conflict. When people ask me how I run the group I tell them that most of the time the discussion runs itself. I'm primarily there to start things off and facilitate.

Although I didn't want the evening to end, eventually we had to wrap things up. I thanked everyone for coming, made sure they knew about the next meeting and the next book, and told them I looked forward to seeing them again. (I'd also had the foresight to start an email list to keep everyone informed of upcoming books and meeting dates, so I now had many new names to add.)

As guys were leaving, they were *still* talking about the book in the library foyer. When I finally got everything in the Conference Room cleaned up, some of them were still talking.

All the way home, I was on a high from the meeting, shaking my head and laughing at how well it had gone. The next challenge was to figure out how to keep it going.

CHAPTER 5

What Now?

I drove home the night of that third meeting still unable to believe it. In my previous teaching career as a band director I often kept notebooks, writing down major events such as concerts, festivals, competitions, etc., detailing what went wrong and what went right. Driving home required that I do this mentally, so I began wondering why so many guys had come out to discuss *The Maltese Falcon* when they had *not* come out for the first two books. Some of my thoughts:

The book had been adapted into a movie they were already familiar with. This was undoubtedly the case with some of the guys since many of them mentioned the film at the meeting. We see this all the time at the library. A new movie comes out based on a book, and suddenly everyone feels compelled to read the book immediately, although before a film adaptation had been announced, the book had probably been sitting on the shelves for years waiting for someone to pick it up. This situation wasn't quite the same thing. The book and the 1941 movie version (clearly the most famous of the three versions) of *The Maltese Falcon* had been out for decades, which probably worked in my favor. The film is part of the lexicon of classic Hollywood, and even if you haven't seen it, you've probably at least heard of it. But I had no way of knowing how many of those guys had seen the film or whether that connection had been responsible for bringing them to the book club.

The title was recognizable. Maybe. This is somewhat related to my first thought about being familiar with the movie. Perhaps some of them *hadn't* seen the movie, but knew the title. Or maybe, since the book was in our Classics section, some of their kids had read it or at least considered it as a choice for required school reading. This was somewhat doubtful since only four or five of the guys in attendance seemed to be of the age to have recently had school-age kids at home.

The book was a hardboiled mystery. Doubtful. Several men in our area read mysteries, but at least a couple of guys in the group mentioned that they normally *don't* read mysteries, hardboiled or otherwise. The hardboiled style of tough, unsentimental crime novels still thrives in mystery fiction (and beyond), and while I was sure some guys were familiar with those books and authors, I didn't exactly see them as fans, so that probably wasn't a huge factor.

My advertising had paid off. I was hoping my comparison of Sam Spade to Michael Connelly's Bosch, Lee Child's Reacher and Robert B. Parker's Spencer would hook a few guys. A couple of those who attended mentioned that they saw the sign and thought about those connections, but maybe they were going to come anyway.

Word of mouth and persistence can do wonders. In the final analysis, I think these last two factors were the most likely reasons thirteen guys showed up to the meeting. Perhaps our little corner of the world in Severna Park, Maryland resembles other parts of America: For most people to be willing to buy into anything new, they have to hear about it from people they know and trust. This clearly was part of the reason we started getting more people. Several guys told me so. I've also seen regulars bring new people with them to meetings. I'm not sure how much word of mouth was responsible for the numbers for *The Maltese Falcon* meeting, but I know from at least a couple of guys that was the case.

Just as important as word of mouth is persistence. I never stopped talking to guys in the library about the book club. Maybe they figured the only way to get me to shut up and stop bothering them was to attend a meeting. Or perhaps people need to see that a program isn't going away and that others are coming to these meetings and enjoying them. Maybe there's something going on and they want to be a part of it.

I think we're all that way, at least to some degree. Before investing our time in any new venture, we want to know it's going to be worth the investment. If we see others enjoying a certain activity, it's entirely possible that we might enjoy it as well. I'm convinced that once people see that something works, they'll consider becoming a part of it. That was my hope going into our fourth meeting.

We had discussed *The Maltese Falcon* in January, which meant the next meetings would occur in March and May. After much thought, I settled on two very different books for those meetings. Keep in mind that I had to choose those titles before the deadline for the next *Happenings* cycle, before I knew we'd have a successful turnout for *The Maltese Falcon*. This may be the most challenging part of a book club, picking titles months in advance before you've really discovered the tastes of the group. Since I was still learning the guys and what they liked, I decided to pick one for them and one for me (a concept that would become important later).

I did this fully conscious of the fact that the numbers for *The Maltese Falcon* may have been a fluke. Wasn't it possible that success had been nothing more than the right book at the right time? Did the guys want more books like that one? Maybe the numbers would drop back down to where they'd been before. I didn't know, but I knew I didn't want to spend time worrying about it. All I was concerned with was picking good books they'd want to read.

During this time I spoke to several people - men and women - who were members of other book clubs, asking them how and who chose their titles. In almost every case, group members chose their books on a rotation system with a different person responsible for selecting a book each month. This idea was one I wanted to consider, but not just yet. If I could establish an unspoken level of quality in our book selections, I felt that the guys would choose books according to that same (or greater) level of quality. Hopefully they would quickly understand that our group wasn't the place for books by the Pattersons and Grishams of the world (not that there's necessarily anything wrong with those books), but for works with more depth, more to discuss. But it was still too early.

When you choose books you like, you start looking at why you like them and how much your tastes line up with those of the group. And if you'd don't really know the group yet, that can be a difficult task. So initially, all you have to go on is your own taste. Recommendations from friends and co-workers are valuable, but you still must do the bulk of the work yourself.

If a book doesn't move me or speak to me in some way, does that mean it won't move or speak to someone else? Not at all. But again you must try to think like your participants. What would they like? What would challenge them? When are they ready for something weighty? Something fun? Something adventurous? Something whimsical? Ask yourself, "Based on what I know about this group, is there any evidence they will enjoy this book?"

Although I wish it were different, my reading tastes are not very broad. I go through phases in my fiction reading. For several years I read nothing but science fiction and fantasy, then later horror. I often dabble in literary fiction, until I run across something I don't feel qualified to attempt. My reading diet usually consists of two or three classics a year, a couple of biographies, a smattering of nonfiction, theology, and graphic novels. The majority of what I read consists of crime fiction and nonfiction works about movies (particularly film noir). All this to say that if I choose *only* books I read and enjoy, it wouldn't be a very big group for very long.

So you need the recommendations of others. It was only a matter of time before I enlisted those recommendations, but for now, the choices were mine alone, for good or bad (and it was some of both).

My thoughts kept drifting back to our second book, *Born to Run*. Perhaps I'd had the right idea with choosing a sports book, but needed to broaden the scope. Michael Lewis's *Moneyball: The Art of Winning an Unfair Game* had been a huge bestseller in 2003, and the movie version was just coming out on DVD, so I figured the title would be on people's minds. I also knew we'd have plenty of copies in circulation. Once again, I would run the risk of having the guys talk more about the movie than the book, but I had a feeling this wouldn't be a huge problem, since the movie was still somewhat new, unlike *The Maltese Falcon*. With a high level of confidence, I chose *Moneyball* for our March book.

The May title was going to be trickier. I wanted another work of fiction, one that dealt with issues these guys could relate to. They could - and did - relate to *The Maltese Falcon*, but probably none of these guys had ever been a private detective trying to deal with a bunch of thieves and cutthroats. Then again, some of them worked in Washington, so maybe…. Just kidding. Mostly.

As much as I love *The Maltese Falcon*, it's an 80-year-old work of fiction. We needed something more current, but also hard-hitting, something that would enable us to reflect on some big issues, meaning-of-life stuff, maybe even with literary merit, and definitely a novel you couldn't ignore.

Several years ago I'd read Cormac McCarthy's *Blood Meridian* (1985) and was absolutely stunned by it. The work is an uncompromisingly brutal novel of western expansion in America, a book hailed as a masterpiece, yet unreadable by some due to its pessimistic tone and relentless graphic depictions of violence. I was confident the book would provide a great amount of discussion, but feared it was too violent, too literary, and too soon for this early in the book club. Not choosing *Blood Meridian* was probably the wisest decision I ever made with the group. That choice was counterbalanced, however, by a near disaster because of the book I chose in its place.

CHAPTER 6

Moneyball and Cormac McCarthy

My hunch about *Moneyball* proved to be right. We had a good turnout for the book, and the discussion was lively[5]. Even this early on I could tell we had several guys who were at least casual sports fans, but up until then had never voiced much of an interest in current sports stories. (It seems we always have a few guys prior to meetings saying things like, "Yeah, the Orioles blew another one..." or something along those lines.) *Moneyball* brought out several questions about whether Oakland A's general manager Billy Beane was a genius, an outlier, or just plain lucky. They tossed around Beane's analyses and theories, wondering if they would work with other teams as well as in other industries, companies, and organizations.

This was a wonderful discussion since it required the reader - like Beane himself - to think outside the box and look at the same information others had available to them, yet find a different way of using it. We had some good comments about how such strategies would or

---

5   I did not consistently begin recording attendance at our meetings until 2013, so I can't say this with any evidence, but I remember having at least eight guys present for the *Moneyball* discussion.

would not work in business, education, the private sector, politics, etc. I'm always a fan of discussions that involve "big concept" thinking as well as unorthodox ways of finding solutions to problems. I wasn't quite sure if the guys would embrace such a discussion, but they all seemed to enjoy the speculative nature of Beane's methods and how they might be applied elsewhere in life.

As expected, a few people mentioned the movie, but since it had just come out on DVD, most of the guys interested in seeing it were on the library holds list. A few had watched it during its theatrical run, but for the most part, those guys kept quiet about it. Although some movie comments are inevitable when discussing a book that's been adapted into a film, I prefer that most of the discussion focus on the book, which is what happened in this case.

The meeting for *Moneyball* also marked the second time a teenager had attended the group. The same father-and-son pair who had joined us for *Born to Run* also came this time, and both seemed to enjoy the discussion. Everyone had something to contribute, and our numbers were solid. The Guys Book Club had now met four times in seven months, and interest was definitely building. So what if the numbers for *Moneyball* weren't quite as good as they had been for *The Maltese Falcon*? I was still encouraged. Things were headed in the right direction and if I didn't screw it up, it looked like a book club for guys might survive and maybe even thrive.

Then Cormac McCarthy walked in. Not literally, of course, but even if he'd been there in the flesh, I'm not sure it would've changed how things went for our May 2012 meeting.

As mentioned in the last chapter, I realized that my preferred McCarthy novel *Blood Meridian* would be too violent, too literary, and too off-putting. The only other novels by McCarthy I had read at the time were *The Road* (2006) and *No Country for Old Men* (2005), later made into an Oscar-winning movie by Joel Coen and Ethan Coen. *No Country for Old Men* is the story of a man named Llewelyn Moss (Josh Brolin in the film) who, while hunting in the West Texas desert, finds the remnants of a drug deal gone wrong, including several dead bodies and a large case filled with money. Leaving the bodies and taking the money, Moss sets into motion a chain of events involving a psychopathic killer named Anton Chigurh (Javier Bardem) and the man trying to bring him to justice, the aging Sheriff Ed Tom Bell (Tommy Lee Jones).

The novel deals with many themes including the nature of evil, the allure of wealth, aging lawmen, the erosion of moral values, and much more. Although far less violent than *Blood Meridian, No Country for Old Men* contains several brutal elements, violent scenes, and philosophies that just aren't very pleasant to think about. Yet I felt the guys could handle most of that.

The element of the book I was most concerned with was the decline of the aging law enforcement officer, which, in a way, stood for a certain type of law-abiding person in a time when lawlessness seems to be gaining the upper hand. It's a concept that finds its summary in the book's title. Would some guys be offended, thinking that the book was nothing more than a cruel reminder of encroaching age and vulnerability? Would it hit too close to home for some? I didn't know for sure, but I would wager that we had at least a few guys in their late-70s and early-80s. How would they feel about the book?

Many of the guys had probably read *The Road*, McCarthy's 2006 post-apocalyptic novel about a father and his son journeying through the ruins of an unnamed cataclysmic event. *The Road* was published to much attention and acclaim even *before* it was chosen as an Oprah's Book Club pick, which immediately skyrocketed its exposure. If these guys had read *The Road*, they no doubt would've been somewhat familiar with McCarthy's style and themes. I decided not to choose *The Road* for two reasons.

One, I didn't care for it. I know I'm swimming upstream on this one, but I felt the book was overly manipulative and predictable. I much prefer Octavia E. Bulter's novel *The Parable of the Sower* (1993), which took the same basic premise and explored it with greater depth, made me feel more for the characters, and forced me to ponder my life much more than McCarthy had with *The Road*. I also wasn't sure I could lead a discussion of a book I really wasn't excited about. (This was not the last time I would struggle with this issue.)

Two, I really felt that *No Country for Old Men* was a better Cormac McCarthy entry point for the guys. Yes, *The Road* was a much more popular (or at least a more widely read) book, but the themes of *No Country* - aging, upholding the law, the encroachment of evil - seemed to be more relevant to the group.

Before we began to discuss *No Country* that evening, I noticed a new face in the group. This guy looked like he was in his mid-30s and seemed very alert and attentive, taking it all in. After a few short announcements, I asked the guys to go around the table and give their names and a few brief thoughts on the book before we got into a deeper discussion.

The first guy to speak said, "I really hated this book," and to be honest, that's all I heard. I can't remember specifically *why* he hated it, but there was no mistaking his antagonism for the novel. Well, I thought, I guess there's always one guy who might hate any book you pick, but at least we got his negative opinion out of the way early. Let's move forward.

But then the next guy also hated the book. And the next guy. And the next.

And on it went, one after another, guys slammed the book for being too violent, bleak, fatalistic, and nihilistic. Several complained that the book offered no hope. They didn't like McCarthy's writing style, his sparse use (or non-use, rather) of punctuation, slang, contractions, you name it. I didn't ask, but I wouldn't have been surprised if there'd been someone who hated the font.

As I'd feared, most of the guys were offended by the utter brutality of the book. Others didn't appreciate the implication (intended by McCarthy or not) that men reach a certain point in their lives that automatically renders them ineffective and useless. I tried to put myself in their shoes. Many of these guys were the same age as (or older than) Sheriff Ed Tom Bell and no doubt saw their own struggles in those of the character. I realized that the book could be interpreted as a "This is what you've got to look forward to" message. An even bleaker message could be taken as "Absolute evil is here and there's not a damn thing you can do about it."

Clearly I had picked the wrong book and was discovering my mistake the hard way. As the minutes dragged on, and the discussion continued, my thoughts turned to the questions, "How can I fix this? Am I going to lose guys over this book?" The group had come up from two or three guys in the beginning to thirteen with *The Maltese Falcon* and since then we'd had a healthy showing of eight to ten guys per meeting. The concern that I had severely injured - or even killed - the Guys Book Club was overwhelming. I didn't know whether I should apologize for the book, defend it, or just cut my losses until next time, but I felt I had to do *something* to address their negativity toward the book.

This bludgeoning of McCarthy's novel (which threatened to surpass the violence described in its pages) went on, but then it was the new guy's turn. He introduced himself (I'll call him John) and said, "Hi everybody, I'm John, and I have to tell you, I absolutely *loved* this book!"

The entire room froze, me included.

John continued. He not only loved the book, he seemed the type of person who gets very animated when discussing something he's passionate about and can't wait to share his thoughts with others. John's response was far more effective than anything I could've said, turning each of the guys' negatives into positives. It wasn't just what he said, it was the way he spoke, in non-confrontational manner, never calling anyone's opinion "wrong," but rather giving the other guys a different perspective to the issues they had with the book.

I'm paraphrasing here, but John asked the guys questions like these: "Do we give up in the face of overwhelming evil? Or do we face it regardless of how we might feel? What was Llewelyn's real motive in stealing the money and why did he keep it when he knew someone was coming after him? Did he really want the best for his family or did selfishness have something to do with it? If so, how much?" Instead of desperation, John found hope in the ending and shared that hope with everyone at the meeting.

This moment had a tremendous impact on the group. You could see it on everyone's face as they considered John's take on the novel: Guys were literally stopping to think about what John had said, considering his points that were so radically different from their own, yet undeniably valid. Although I'm not sure John changed anyone's opinion of the novel, no one who spoke after him attacked it in the same way as before. Some of the remaining members conceded many of John's points, but still didn't care for the book.

Yet I'm sure others began to see John's point of view and appreciate the items he brought up that the book is a reflection on life, death, belief, and so much more. I'll be honest: A part of me was delighted that John was there to help validate my own thoughts on the book, but what was more important was the fact that, in the midst of an almost unanimous dislike for the novel, many now thought about it in ways they hadn't before.

I suppose a book club can be fun if everyone in the group agrees that a certain book is good (or bad), but opposing viewpoints provide for more memorable discussions. That meeting also showed me (and the other guys) that for some questions there are no "right" answers. Although everyone in the room is reading the same book, each person is going to look at it in a variety of ways, bringing something different and unique to the table.

After all these years, I continue to find that aspect of the book club enormously exciting. Although I'll hear various thoughts and opinions from at least two or three guys (either in person or via email) before each meeting, I never really know how the discussion is going to go or whether the majority will like or dislike a book. As the group's facilitator, you think you know which directions the discussion will take and try to prepare accordingly. But anything can happen. You can attempt to script discussions, but you just have to let them take their own course. I think the guys appreciate that as well.

Back to *No Country for Old Men*. John had saved the day in a manner of speaking. It's one thing for me as the group's facilitator to "swim upstream" against the opinions of the group, but it's something else to have at least one other person swimming with you. I kept wondering what would've happened that night had John *not* been there. I didn't exactly expect anarchy or anything like that, but I'll admit it would've been challenging had mine been the only voice in support of the book.

After the meeting John came up to me and told me how much he enjoyed both the book and the discussion. I thanked him for coming and for voicing such strong enthusiasm for the novel and for not being afraid to speak up in its defense. But I was crestfallen when he told me that his first meeting would also be his last: John had recently taken a job in another part of the state and would no longer be living in Anne Arundel County. The *No Country for Old Men* meeting was the only one he ever attended.

CHAPTER 7

Patterns Emerge and a Request is Made

Despite an almost universal dislike among the group for *No Country for Old Men*, my level of excitement for our upcoming meeting led me to believe our next book could be the one to make everyone forget our near disastrous experience with Cormac McCarthy. That book was *Destiny of the Republic: A Tale of Madness, Medicine, and the Murder of a President* by Candice Millard, the story of the assassination of the 20th President of the United States, James A. Garfield (1831-1881).

When *Destiny of the Republic* was first published, I was immediately drawn to it, remembering the scant attention my high school American History class had given Garfield's presidency and extraordinary death. I knew he'd been assassinated, but either couldn't remember the details behind the killing or had never been told of them. The fault is probably my own, since I had an excellent history teacher (my aunt, Margaret Richardson, who taught history for 32 years; her own story could fill a book). Millard had obviously conducted meticulous research on the topic, which, in itself, was quite impressive, but she also knows how to tell a compelling story.

Like others I'd spoken to about the book, I literally couldn't put it down until the last page was turned.

Several factors made this a good pick for the group. First, I knew from talking to the guys individually and from their recommendations that we had many history buffs in the group. The only real history book we had read up to that point had been *Unbroken*, and only a few guys had attended that first meeting. If history was indeed one of the guys' favorite subjects, *Destiny of the Republic* could prove a winner.

Second, Millard's readable writing style and solid research would no doubt win the guys over. In talking about the book to several people, I frequently compared her style to that of David McCullough, another popular writer of history many guys had brought up in previous meetings. Like McCullough, Millard has the rare ability to put you in the mindset of hearing a well-told tale while sitting around a campfire. It's a story filled with historical authenticity, yet the research never bogs down the narrative, but rather enhances it and gives it credence.

Millard's book also shares connections with another work that several of the guys had read on their own, Erik Larson's *The Devil in the White City.* We live in a time where you constantly hear product comparisons such as "If you liked _____, you'll like _____," or "Customers who bought _____ also bought _____," but in making such comparisons, you must exercise caution. The similarities of the two books was probably enough, but after I talked to several guys about the subject of *Destiny of the Republic*, they were solidly on board.

Two "firsts" happened with *Destiny of the Republic*. Weeks before the meeting, a few guys had come up to me to tell me how much they enjoyed the book. That situation had happened perhaps once or twice in the days leading up to a meeting, but now several guys were telling me how much they loved *Destiny* and how they couldn't wait to discuss it. Of course I was delighted to hear this. It told me that guys weren't waiting until the last minute to read the book, that they were really engaged and highly anticipated the upcoming discussion.

It also created a problem I wasn't prepared for, one Heather had warned me about before the club even got off the ground: having enough copies. *Destiny of the Republic* was so popular that all the print copies were soon checked out, and people had to place holds for it. In a way, this really wasn't much of a surprise. After all, this was not Millard's first work. In 2005 she had published her debut *The River of Doubt: Theodore Roosevelt's Darkest Journey* about Roosevelt's 1913-14 expedition of the Amazon rainforest with the Brazilian explorer Cândido Mariano da Silva Rondonof. That book was a bestseller, but many of the guys (as well as our library patrons in general) didn't yet know about that title or Millard. Initially *Destiny of the Republic* moved steadily from the library shelves, but after it had been around for a few weeks, word of mouth spread like crazy. You couldn't find a copy anywhere.

My concern was that many of the guys wouldn't be able to read the book in time for the meeting. I can't remember who it was, but one of my coworkers told me that we could request additional copies of a book if it was a current title, which *Destiny of the Republic* clearly was. At the time, this was the normal operational procedure in our system when many people are on hold for a new book: Materials Management (Mat Man) will normally purchase one additional copy for every seven people waiting. (That number has fluctuated over the years, but it's usually between seven and ten.)

With book clubs, the situation is a bit different. Again, the title in question must be a new release. Our system isn't going to purchase more copies of an older book that will probably just sit on the shelf after the book club is finished with it. The Mat Man staff understandably want to make sure library funds are spent wisely on materials that will continue to circulate beyond the one-time book club selection.

I didn't want to make a habit of such a request, but I made it this time, hoping that it was far enough in advance that (1) the extra copies would arrive on time and, (2) the guys would have time to read them before the meeting. Everything worked out well. The copies were ordered and the guys (as well as the general library public) didn't have to wait very long. Crisis averted. As an added plus, people continued to want to read the book well after the book club, so those extra copies got even more mileage.

As I suspected, the guys were totally engaged in the book, not only with its subject matter but also Millard's writing style: approachable, compelling, and well-researched. That combination is difficult to find. Again, David McCullough is probably our leading example of such work, but Millard is quickly catching up to him.

As I also suspected, many of the guys wanted to know what else Millard had written. I told them about her first book *The River of Doubt,* and I believe one person had read it but hadn't made the connection that it was written by the same author as *Destiny of the Republic.* Suddenly everyone wanted to read *The River of Doubt* (which we did a couple of years later) and anything else Millard wrote. (We also read and discussed Millard's 2016 book *Hero of the*

Empire, making Millard the most-read author of the Guys Book Club.)

The other thing I took away from that meeting was the overwhelming hunger and thirst these guys have for books on American history. Something came alive at that meeting, and although many of the guys had been interested and actively vocal in previous discussions, the participation grew more spirited that night. Maybe it had something to do with President Garfield's story being one they hadn't heard much about, lending an element of buried historical treasure to the book, or maybe it struck a chord for some other reason.

By that time, the book club had drawn in several veterans, so I'm sure that accounted for some of the interest in history. It seemed I had found other guys who genuinely enjoy reading and talking about historical events. Not only did they enjoy discussing them, they were (and are) expert in making intelligent connections to how historical events have parallels to current situations. I'll explore that further as we talk more about books of a historical nature, but their reaction to *Destiny of the Republic* was something I keep tucked away in my mind when choosing future books.

At one of our meetings (It must have been at the *Moneyball* meeting, our fourth) the book discussion ended, and one of the guys asked, "Andy, is there any reason why we couldn't meet *every* month instead of every other month?" Other guys around the table nodded and said they'd also like monthly meetings.

As you might imagine, I felt both delighted and a little unnerved at the prospect of meeting every month: delighted that the guys enjoyed the books and discussions enough to want to make it a more regular occurrence, but concerned that I would be able to handle reading, choosing, and coming up with a structure for the book club on a monthly basis. (By this time I had also started working on my Master of Library and Information Science degree, which took up much of my free time.)

Going monthly presented implications for both me and the group. As for myself, I'd have to do much more reading. Up to this point, I'd mostly picked books I'd already read or was familiar with. This was an advantage in many ways. I knew the books, but with the group covering one book every other month, I had plenty of time to re-read and review the book before each meeting. Six books a year was very doable. I wasn't so sure I could handle 12 books a year *and* graduate level courses.

Since I would be choosing three books per *Happenings* cycle, my task would be to constantly have titles ready to go for the group. This meant keeping track of books I'd read in the past as well as the nearly impossible task of looking at the constant flow of new books. I don't even have time to read all the books that interest me on a personal level, much less those that would interest the group, so I knew I'd have to read many reviews as well as talk to co-workers and other serious readers.

After the Guys Book Club had met only a couple of times, I began keeping a running list of books I thought the group might like. The titles on that list usually ran to at least a dozen, and I kept adding to it frequently. It also became a regular occurrence for guys to recommend books to me at least once a week. My goal was to always read at least a couple of chapters from each recommendation, but after a while their suggestions kept coming at such a fast pace that I could no longer do even that. (Audiobooks helped, if they were available for those suggested titles, but I was still playing catch-up.) And this was when we were meeting every *other* month.

Add to this every book lover's problem: Publishers continue cranking out new books every month whether you're ready for them or not. How in the world was I going to be able to keep up with it all?

The best decision seemed to be keeping up with my list of books that I was familiar with, drawing from that list primarily, at least for a while. If I could get five or six previously read books lined up, that would give me some breathing room to pick newer titles and to examine the books guys were recommending to me.

The next task was to trim down the recommended titles. One of the things that helped was checking the number of copies we had of any suggested title in the system. If one of the guys recommended a book that was several years old, it was likely we wouldn't have enough copies for it to be chosen. If that was the case, there was usually no need to pursue that title any further.

I'd also ask the guys recommending books *why* they thought their particular title would be a good fit for the group. In many cases, the book was a biography or had to do with history, both of which were usually worth exploring. In other cases, guys were coming up with good titles, but ones that were too similar to ones we had recently read. In such cases, I told them their choices were good, but too close to a book we'd just discussed. Keep that one in your pocket for a while, I'd tell them.

Choosing back-to-back titles that were too similar or picking books from the same subject area always presents a challenge. As soon as you've chosen a great book on a certain topic, you'll often find another great book on the same topic and can't (or shouldn't) program them one after the other. So planning gets a little more complicated.

Most of the guys understood the need for my development of some type of criteria for our choices and were fine with it. I always appreciated their suggestions, even when they didn't quite fit the group or weren't the right book at the right time. There were simply too many suggestions and recommendations for me to read even one full chapter from each book they recommended, and the problem was that most of their recommendations were good.

I also had to take a close look at what was really being said in some of the suggested books. Did the author have an ax to grind? Was the work one that was highly politically charged toward one side or the other? I still wanted to avoid discussing politics and religion outright, but I knew that eventually books on those topics would come up.

Some titles were easier to dismiss than others. It became quite easy to eliminate books for reasons of availability, politics and/or religion, and simply knowing the general interest level of the guys. I felt I was still able to keep up, but it was going to be a struggle, especially with school.

Heather and Karen were both delighted that the club was catching on, but were concerned with putting too much on my plate. I'm not sure who suggested it (maybe both of them), but we decided not to have the book club meet in June or July, since the primary focus of those months would be our Summer Reading Club, always a busy time. Then we could start back in August on a monthly basis if that's what I wanted to do. That seemed like a wonderful idea. Those summer months would allow me some extra time to plan for the upcoming monthly schedule, possibly even allowing me to choose books six months or more in advance. That would certainly give me some much-needed breathing room.

There never was any question of what I *wanted* to do, which was to meet monthly with the group. The guys were enjoying it, I was enjoying it, and we were picking up new members on a consistent basis. I already had a fairly long list of books that I wanted to read with the group, so I had accumulated something of a stockpile for several months. Prep time would be minimal.

I made up my mind. We were going monthly.

CHAPTER 8

Bill Bryson and the Long Tale

After the near disaster that was *No Country for Old Men*, the Guys Book Club enjoyed several good meetings in a row. As already mentioned in the previous chapter, *Destiny of the Republic* was a big hit. We followed that with *In Defense of Food: An Eater's Manifesto* by Michael Pollan, and *Outliers: The Story of Success* by Malcolm Gladwell, both of which were hugely popular with the guys and generated excellent discussions. One guy was so taken with *In Defense of Food* that he decided to change many of his own eating habits. "I don't know how long I can do it," he said, "but I'm sure gonna try!" After our discussion of *Outliers*, many of the group's members asked if we could read and discuss Gladwell's other books.

What the group liked about both the Pollan and Gladwell books is how universal they are. Regardless of whether you enjoy reading about the science of food or what some people have done to become enormously successful, these two books covered topics that concerned everyone at the meeting. Everybody eats and most everybody wants to know how people succeed. These discussions went far beyond the "Wow, that was a great book" realm and moved into areas of deeper thought, potentially life-changing stuff. The guys were starting to think about the implications of both books what they meant for their lives and futures. Not bad for a book club...

With respect to the Pollan book, many of the guys (including me) realized that one of Pollan's points - that our fruit-and-vegetable-deficient Western diet is largely responsible for the general poor health of many in this country - was both valid and urgent. *And we could do something about it.* Yet a few members were skeptical about the author's findings, questioning some of his statements and suggestions.

This contrast in opinion was exciting, since discussions in which people disagree with or at least question aspects of the books are far more interesting than full-on acceptance. Members asked questions, broached subjects, and gave opinions, all with a sense of courtesy and decorum. The same happened with the Gladwell book. You could see the wheels turning in the minds of several of the guys. In many cases their thinking was being challenged, gently and in a good way, by these books. Yet no one felt threatened or isolated, at least as far as I could tell. This was thrilling! I just love to hear comments like "I hadn't thought about that," or "This has really given me something to think about." These guys were challenging each other in ways that weren't examples of one-upmanship, but rather exploration and intellectual curiosity.

Perhaps the most exciting aspect of these discussions was the willingness of each member to consider something new, whether that came from the words of the author(s) or the comments from other members. I'm not sure how much of that sprang up from the group and how much was already a part of those guys' thinking processes to begin with. People who read are generally more open to considering differences of opinion and thought. Maybe these guys had already brought such attributes with them, but I hoped that just being in the group helped guys consider different ways of thinking about a subject.

When I chose those two books, I had hoped for such discussions. Maybe we had been together long enough to start feeling comfortable conversing over such matters, especially in a respectful way when disagreements arose. Yet after two such books, we might need something a little lighter.

It was during this time that I decided to revisit a book my wife and I had enjoyed reading several years earlier. *A Walk in the Woods* is Bill Bryson's nonfiction account of a mid-life crisis that resulted in his desire to hike the entire Appalachian Trail, all 2,190 miles of it. The memoir is filled with reflections on life from a man then in his mid-40s, but also focuses on nature, ecology, sociology, and the hiking culture. Plus, it's often hilarious. After having it sit on my shelf for years, I picked it up again, read a few chapters, and immediately felt it would be a hit with the group.

In the weeks and days leading up to the meeting I'd spoken to several guys who'd previously enjoyed the book and were looking forward to reading it again. Even the ones who were encountering it for the first time would share with me some of the humor and/or enlightenment they'd discovered in its pages. There was no doubt in my mind this could turn into one of our best discussions ever.

But what happened was a nightmare. Not the kind of nightmare you'd experience upon meeting a hungry bear on the Appalachian Trail or forgetting to bring along an essential piece of hiking equipment, but still a nightmare.

The meeting began well. To kick things off, I produced a postcard I'd received just a few days earlier which I read for the guys and passed around. For some strange reason, I had been in the habit of contacting the living authors of the books we were reading and asking them if they would like to join us for our book club discussion. (More about this in Chapter 11.) I had contacted Bill Bryson's publisher via snail mail, expecting no response. (Contacting authors had become something of a perfunctory act for me. Again, more on this in Chapter 11.) But this time I received a postcard from Bryson, mailed from his home in the UK, which stated that while he was unable to attend, he was delighted that we had chosen his book and wished us the best. It was, of course, signed by Bryson. The guys were clearly impressed that a real live author - especially one of Bryson's stature and popularity - had contacted us.

After that bit of fun, I began the meeting proper by asking if anyone had ever hiked part or all of the Appalachian Trail. Only a couple of hands went up. Although we had some very athletic guys in the group, no one had hiked the entire trail, but at least two (including myself) had hiked at least a part of it. (In my case, I'd hiked a *very* short part of it in Georgia.) Some of the men who had some hiking experience, the Appalachian Trail or otherwise, compared their experiences to those of Bryson and his traveling companion Katz. Guys were making comments on the book, sharing their experiences, and all was well until a new guy started to speak. I'll call him Ed.

Ed was a large man, not fat, but a big guy who looked like he could've once played linebacker for a good college football team, maybe even pro, a man in his mid-40s or early-50s, still in good shape. He sat near the door at the far end of the table, almost as far away from my seat as you could get. After the discussion had been going for a good 15 or 20 minutes, Ed began relating a story about one of his own hikes. (If I'm remembering correctly, it *wasn't* a hike on the Appalachian Trail.)

Now understand that Ed didn't start this travelogue by announcing that he was undertaking an anecdote or a story, and *certainly* not an epic tale of Homeric proportions, He just started talking.

And he kept talking. And talking. And talking, relating the microscopic details of one of his hikes, including his surroundings, what he had packed, the weather conditions, barometric pressure, isobars, soil textures, you name it. Throughout his tale, Ed's eyes never met those of any of the other guys. Instead, he focused on the table, the ceiling, anywhere but the other faces in the room. He was in his own little world and was clearly holding court. Maybe this was the first time he'd ever told this story, or perhaps he felt it was the appropriate audience and context for his tale, or maybe he'd told it countless times, but that night he was telling it *all*. I began to think I should call either the Guinness Book of World Records or the Johns Hopkins School of Medicine because this guy didn't pause for a single breath in what seemed like ten minutes. There was literally no way to get a word in because Ed's hiking manifesto was one enormous stream-of-consciousness sentence worthy of James Joyce, one that seemed as if it was never going to end.

I looked around the room, thinking, *Maybe it's just me. Maybe this isn't going on as long as I think it is.* Initially I saw guys watching Ed, listening attentively, respectfully. There were no anxious looks on their faces, no eyes widening in disbelief. Maybe it was just me.

And the story kept on going with Ed showing no signs of flagging. This wasn't a story, it was its own multivolume travelogue and we were on perhaps page seven or eight of what I feared would be the *War and Peace* of hiking stories.

Looking around the room, I noticed other guys were now start-ing to fidget, rubbing their chins, looking down at the table, clearing their throats, glancing at their watches, looking at their phones, looking at *me*. I knew I had to do something. I'd always wanted the guys to be able to speak freely, but this was getting ridiculous, approaching filibuster territory.

But how I could stop this guy without being rude? It was Ed's first time with the group, and while I certainly wanted him to have his turn, I had to let him know that this was a group that allows everyone who wants to talk an opportunity to do so. He clearly wasn't allowing anyone else to do that. Maybe it was an honest mistake. Or maybe he was a blowhard who just didn't care. I didn't know, but I knew I had to do something fast.

How long this went on, I can't be sure (probably not as long as it seemed to me at the time), but finally I interrupted Ed in mid-sen-tence. "Ed, that's a great story, but I'm going to stop you for a moment because I think we've got some other guys who want to comment."

In that moment, I *prayed* there would be *someone* besides Ed who had a comment to make, anyone that would deliver us from this never-ending travelogue. I waited for what seemed an hour for some brave soul to rescue us all.

Thankfully someone did. I can't remember who it was, but that guy has my everlasting gratitude. What this guy said was some-thing along the lines of "I want to mention a part of the book that connected with me," and then related it. Waves of relief flooded over me. Other than walking into an empty cell on a tour of Alcatraz, I've never been in prison, but it felt like my cell had just been opened and I'd been set free. The first thing I did, after exhaling, was look at Ed.

He seemed a little perturbed, as if someone had just unplugged his electric shaver before he could finish shaving. Ed wasn't looking at the guy who was speaking, but rather down at the table, directly in front of him, scowling. With his mouth closed, he began silently moving his lips as if he was still talking or practicing for the next time he'd be allowed to speak. Concern grew in me that this was just a temporary reprieve, that - Lord help us all - his previous recitation had only been Part One. Or even worse, a *prelude* to Part One.

My thankfulness for those guys who stepped up with comments is endless. Again, I wish I could remember who they were; I'd give each of them a medal of valor. They truly kept the meeting from going off the rails, and they did it with class.

And then Ed began speaking again.

But something was different this time. A bit of the bravado was missing, although some of it clearly remained. I can't remember if he continued from where he'd left off in his previous story or if it was a new adventure, but it really didn't matter. Like his first contribution, it had nothing to do with the book, but rather his own hiking experiences. This time, however, the longer he spoke, the less conviction his tale carried. He was on autopilot, but low on fuel. True, he had lost a lot of altitude and perhaps was looking for one long, distant runway, but he still had some gas left in the tank.

Something in the way he now spoke told me he was defeated. Like the first time, Ed seemed to want to keep going and going, yet he didn't have the same amount of vigor. This time, all I had to do was look around the room and find just one guy who was making eye contact with me. I found one. Again, I can't remember who it was, but let's say it was a guy named John. As soon as I saw John's eyes, I simply said, "John, you've got something?" And John did.

And that was it for Ed. He was done. Throughout the rest of the meeting, he remained silent. The other guys continued discussing the book normally, and it appeared everyone was back to having a good time. Except for Ed.

I didn't see this as an "I win, you lose" situation. I simply wanted other guys to have the opportunity to speak. Although those minutes had been uncomfortable, I didn't have anything personal against Ed. He seemed like an okay guy; maybe he just enjoyed talking about himself. Lots of people do. Maybe he was the type of guy no one paid attention to at work or at home. Maybe all he needed was the opportunity to talk. Giving him that opportunity was fine, but only to a point. I had other guys in the room who also deserved that opportunity and to allow him to continue to try to dominate the conversation - regardless of the reason - was unfair to everyone.

When the meeting ended, Ed was, if I remember correctly, the first one to leave. The sense of relief I had that the meeting hadn't been a total loss gave way to something deeper. I wondered if Ed was simply seeking people to talk to. No, that wasn't exactly it. He wasn't *conversing* with the other guys, but relating his own experiences to them, which I suppose could be his way of interacting with people. As I mentioned earlier, perhaps he had no one else in his life who would listen to him. I felt that maybe I should've said something to him, but I didn't know what that would be.

I learned long ago as a teacher that when students in my class disobeyed, broke the rules, or caused various shenanigans, it probably had nothing to do with me. In many cases, there are problems going on before they ever get to your classroom. It could be they're new students and really don't know the rules yet. Or maybe they're just testing the waters, seeing what the limits are. But sometimes

those students aren't breaking the rules just to break the rules. There's something else going on in their lives, something they aren't sure how to handle. Breaking the rules can simply be a way to get attention. But sometimes it's a cry for help.

I'm not trying to play armchair psychiatrist here. First of all, I'm not qualified to do so, and second, I wouldn't want the job. Yet sometimes there's something there. I didn't know what might've been going on with Ed, but at the very least I should've spoken to him and thanked him for coming to the meeting. I don't know, maybe he would've said something, maybe not. I'll never know now.

After that meeting I would see Ed come into the library from time to time. He was always alone, always looked at the displays of new fiction and nonfiction, and never came anywhere close to the Information Desk. My mind struggled with whether to approach him and at least say hello. I'm sorry to say I never did. Maybe that one bad experience kept me from talking to him. Perhaps my fears got the better of me, keeping me from making that first step that could've led to a better understanding of the guy. I regret not doing so. I decided that in the future I would try to do a better job of seeking to understand problem situations and the people behind them. It was ironic that I could walk up to any guy in the library and start talking about the Guys Book Club, but hesitated to initiate a one-on-one conversation with someone who had made the effort to attend, someone who stepped out on a limb and maybe even gotten out of his comfort zone to join us. Even with that problematic meeting, Ed had taken the first step, but I had not taken the next one.

CHAPTER 9

Choosing the Books

As I mentioned earlier, I chose all the titles for the Guys Book Club from the very beginning until late 2015. Input from the guys themselves was always a primary consideration, but I also leaned heavily on all my other book-loving friends and co-workers. I considered every book I read, determining if it would be a good fit for the club. My own personal reading covers a little bit of everything, fiction and nonfiction, but no one can read everything, so I depend on a wide variety of sources including reviews from readers I trust. (You must be careful with reviews on Amazon and Goodreads; some people don't like *anything* and others give five-star ratings to *everything*.)

The guys always gave me suggestions, and I tried to read at least the first few chapters of each recommended book. In some cases, guys would (with the best of intentions) simply suggest their favorite books, sometimes based on fond memories of a title they'd read decades ago. Others recommended books on certain issues that they felt were important or timely. I seriously considered each work and would usually get back to them with responses ranging from "I think this is a great title, but probably not a good fit for most of the guys" to "This is great. We'll do it!"

The process felt like what an editor goes through in accepting or rejecting manuscripts, and in a way, I suppose that's exactly what I was doing. But I'd read each suggestion with the following in mind: (1) Would this book provide opportunity for a good discussion? and (2) Would this book polarize people?

One of my primary considerations was to stick to my original rule not to choose a book that was currently political or having to do with religion. I think I did a pretty good job of holding to that rule until one member recommended *Power, Faith, and Fantasy: America in the Middle East: 1776 to the Present* by Michael B. Oren. Wow, here was a book that was about both politics *and* religion, *plus* it covered the modern day. But after reading just the first two chapters, I knew we had to read it. The book was too well written and researched, too important to dismiss. That meeting also led to one of our finest discussions. Yet, oddly enough, we haven't tackled that many books that focus on current political or religious issues since.

Like *Power, Faith, and Fantasy*, many of the suggested books were either unfamiliar to me or they simply weren't on my radar. Several such titles I ended up choosing, among them *Team of Rivals: The Political Genius of Abraham Lincoln* by Doris Kearns Goodwin, *Flash Boys: A Wall Street Revolt* by Michael Lewis, and others. I read those books (or at least their first chapters) and decided each would be a great fit for the group. Again, no one can read everything.

It soon became clear that not only could I not read everything the guys were suggesting, I couldn't even read the first chapters of all the books they proposed. Part of this situation coincided with my promotion from Library Associate to Librarian 1 in 2013. (In our system at the time, a Library Associate was a reference librarian with a bachelor's degree in something other than library science.

A Librarian 1 had earned the Master of Library and Information Science degree and was responsible for more facets of library work. Our structures changed in 2021, but much of these designations still hold true.)

Moving to a Librarian 1 position wasn't so bad, but Librarian 1 staff are also in charge of one specific part of the library, usually on a two-year rotation: overall local library collection, local building and facilities, outreach, and programming. In 2015 I was placed in charge of programming, which covers all children's programming (including three different levels of early literacy storytime programs), teen and adult programming, and special events. The job also involved promoting those events, helping develop new ones, and being the first line of defense for people who come to the library with great (and not-so-great) ideas for library programs. Several staff members helped me with this, but it was a lot to handle. With all this going on, I needed to let go of something and made the decision to leave some of the responsibility of choosing of the books up to the guys.

I worked out a system that would allow them to vote on any books they wanted as long as they were in the library system and we had enough copies. They would send me an email with their nomination(s) with a short note explaining why they thought their book(s) would be a good fit for the club.

Each time I received an email recommendation, I checked to see how many copies we had in the system and how many more we might reasonably be able to purchase. If we had only a handful of copies (five or fewer) of a title, or none, that book was a "no." If it was between six and ten copies, it was possible; I just had to contact the Materials Management department at Library Headquarters and see if it was possible to get more copies *if* it was a fairly current book still in print[6]. In some ways, this process still took some time, but it was nothing compared to reading the first chapters of several books.

As I mentioned in Chapter 2, all libraries in our system are required to send program information, including book club titles, to library headquarters for inclusion in *Happenings* several months in advance, which meant I imposed two deadlines for the guys: a nomination deadline and a voting deadline. When the nomination deadline ended, I sent out an email with all the nominated titles and authors, how many copies we had in the system in various formats, and the descriptions given by the guys. I also told the guys that if they didn't give *any* description for the book(s) they nominated, people likely wouldn't vote for it. Some guys gave great descriptions; others gave none.

When nominations went out, guys had a week to vote for their top three choices. Each first choice received three votes, second choices two, third choices one. The only other rule was that if a book had been nominated without being chosen for three cycles, that book was finished.

The first time we voted for November and December 2015 and January 2016 titles. When the votes were tabulated, I was stunned with the results. The top three vote-getters were all works of fiction. Not only that, these were *not* novels you would typically associate with men's reading habits, which generally lean toward nonfiction. Those titles were *The Cellist of Sarajevo* by Steven Galloway (November 2015), *Pride and Prejudice* by Jane Austen (December

---

6 The policy has changed since then. For any book club title, the system must own at least 10 copies (or combination of any kind: print and/or digital).

2015), and *Orphan Train* by Christina Baker Kline (January 2016), not exactly rugged, tough-guy titles.

To put this in perspective, the Guys Book Club had previously discussed a total of 45 books, 30 of which had been nonfiction. Here were three works of fiction in a row. After I stopped scratching my head, I began to wonder how this had happened.

How many of these books had the guys actually read, and how many were "suggested" to them, perhaps by reviews they'd read in the paper or maybe even recommendations from their wives. I also wondered if these were what I call "buzzword" books.

While I was very excited about reading and discussing *Pride and Prejudice* (which I had read before), neither *The Cellist of Sarajevo* nor *Orphan Train* were titles I would've chosen. I am normally suspicious of any book, movie, TV show, or any other form of artistic expression that captures the attention and adoration of the culture at large, so those two "buzzword" books were not on my radar, and I'll be honest: I wasn't looking forward to reading them. But I thought about all the books that I had chosen for the guys in the past, books that *they* probably weren't all that excited about reading, but read anyway. I decided to give them a try.

The Cellist of Sarajevo was nominated and led by a guy named Bill Saur. Unknown to me at the time, Bill had spent a significant amount of time working in Sarajevo and knew the area very well. As he led the discussion, Bill expertly led us not only through the book itself, but also through the city of Sarajevo, relaying cultural, social, and historical information that we wouldn't have otherwise known, facts that helped bring us all deeper into the story. Bill's leadership with this title gave me a new appreciation of a book that I had enjoyed only on a surface level. More importantly, the guys at the meeting were also engaged, finding that Bill's personal story made the book come alive for them in ways it probably wouldn't have otherwise.

The most important thing that the guys took away from *Pride and Prejudice* was a better understanding of the female point of view. It took several of the guys significant time and effort to get past the attitudes, social manners, and writing style of the period, but once they did, most of them found the book rewarding, if not enlightening. This was more than a bunch of guys getting in touch with their "feminine" sides; it really was a revelation for some of them in understanding women, not just women of that historical era, but also contemporary women. I shared some of these moments with my branch manager and other coworkers. I don't know if their silence stemmed from joy, disbelief, or both, but they were just as stunned as I was. And, I reminded them, this is a book that *the guys themselves* voted for!

Most everyone at the meeting for *Orphan Train* agreed that the story of orphans transported from the crowded orphanages of the Eastern U.S. to more rural areas was far more interesting than the novel's execution of the story. (This happens from time to time: the guys become more interested in the subject of a novel rather than the author's writing. This doesn't necessarily mean the quality of the writing is inferior.)

One group member discussed how the book affected him, since he grew up an orphan. While many of them enjoyed it, most of the guys felt the novel provided an impetus to read more about the history of the Orphan Train Movement.

Again, these three works of fiction were all books the guys had voted in. I had nothing to do with it. It was still surprising that a group that seemed to gravitate toward nonfiction works had chosen three novels in a row. While two out of the three were books I wouldn't have picked, I felt good that the job of selecting the books was totally in the hands of the group. Allowing them full control over the titles freed me up tremendously. I was glad to have the task of choosing the books taken off my plate.

But not everyone was glad.

After this first round of books chosen exclusively by the guys, a couple of the members (separately) came up to me complaining about the book choices. These were guys who generally preferred nonfiction over fiction, but there was more to their complaint. They thought the books were too light, too trendy. I told them that I understood their feelings but would like for them to give this method more time. We'd only had the guys choosing the books for one quarter and should give it more of a chance. They agreed to do so.

The next round of books they chose was about as different from their first selections as you could get. These were all nonfiction titles covering specific periods of history: *The Boys in the Boat: Nine Americans and Their Epic Quest for Gold at the 1936 Berlin Olympics* by Daniel James Brown, *Operation Nemesis: The Assassination Plot that Avenged the Armenian Genocide* by Eric Bogosian, and *Undaunted Courage: Meriwether Lewis, Thomas Jefferson, and the Opening of the American West* by Stephen Ambrose.

Each of those meetings seemed to spark a different level of participation and excitement. You could just see it on their faces: guys were more engaged, more enthusiastic, more willing to contribute. These were meetings that could've gone well beyond our allotted hour and sometimes did. It seemed the guys who had complained earlier about the selections were feeling better about things. Several works of fiction had been nominated for this round, but it seemed the majority were having none of it. Nonfiction was back, and everything was right with the Guys Book Club.

And then it wasn't.

The problems and complaints didn't all resurface at once. In our next round of books, we enjoyed good discussions of *The Finest Hours: The True Story of the U.S. Coast Guard's Most Daring Sea Rescue* by Michael J. Tougias and Casey Sherman (led by Nino Martini) and *Midnight in the Garden of Good and Evil* by John Berendt (led by Paul Stillwell). Yet the next book in this cycle, *The Nightingale* by Kristin Hannah, brought out some major complaints.

Many appreciated the book's setting and time period, the story of two sisters in France at the dawn of World War II, but cared little for the actual story itself, which some considered too sentimental. Others overlooked the book's faults and embraced the story for what it is, but the majority didn't care for the book. It was after this meeting that I received the most complaints about how the books were being chosen.

Maybe the problems had to do with the works of fiction we were choosing. In talking to the guys individually, I discovered that it wasn't that they didn't like fiction, they just didn't like *these particular* works of fiction that had been chosen. These things seemed to come in waves; looking at the next round of voting, I saw that there were no novels on the list for the next three months. Crisis avoided.

Or not.

A few months later, just when I thought everything was fine, guys began coming to me with a different concern. A couple of the members pointed out that we had chosen several books in a row that had to do with war, killing, death, deception, and terrorism. We'd chosen *Eisenhower in War and Peace* by Jean Edward Smith, *The Mathews Men: Seven Brothers and the War Against Hitler's U-Boats* by William Geroux, *A Spy Among Friends: Kim Philby and the Great Betrayal* by Ben Macintyre, and *Black Flags: The Rise of ISIS* by Joby Warrick.

They were right: those books not only contained a tremendous amount of war and conflict, some of them were also tough to read emotionally. (At least two guys told me how depressed they felt after reading *A Spy Among Friends,* which chronicles Kim Philby's extraordinarily high levels of lying, betrayal, and deception.) It was too much for several of them. I had to admit those books were beginning to take a toll on me as well.

And things weren't looking much brighter beyond that. Our next three books had to do with war (*Hero of the Empire: The Boer War, a Daring Escape, and the Making of Winston Churchill* by Candice Millard), terrorism (*Playing to the Edge: American Intelligence in the Age of Terror* by Michael V. Hayden), and Hitler's rise to power as experienced by America's Ambassador to Germany (*In the Garden of Beasts: Love, Terror, and an American Family in Hitler's Berlin* by Erik Larson). Not exactly good times at the Guys Book Club.

What could be done about it? If I went back to choosing all the books myself, I didn't think I'd have much time to do anything else, and with my overall programming responsibilities, I didn't see how I could pick and prepare twelve books a year (at least not at a very high level). Plus I really didn't want to take the guys' voices out of the picture. I valued their opinions in choosing the books as much as I valued their opinions and thoughts during our meetings.

I sent an email to the guys, describing the dilemma and asking for their suggestions. The overwhelming majority of the guys agreed that we were reading too many books they felt were too dark and depressing *and* that we were reading them too often. Only one guy said that he really liked the books we were reading, which surprised me. He related this to me in person, so I asked him exactly what he meant by that.

(I'm paraphrasing here.) "I realize that there's so much evil in the world, both in our own times and in the past," he said. "Reading books like these is one of the ways I can deal with all that evil, to know that someone else is bothered by it besides me. It gives me hope." Although I understood and respected his viewpoint, his was the only voice in full support of the books we were choosing.

Yet I wondered… If so many guys were opposed to those books, why did they continue to get voted in? I asked this of several of the guys during one-on-one conversations I'd have with them at the Info Desk or out on the floor of the library.

Most of them said that they recognized several of these books as ones they knew we *should* read and discuss, titles that were important in showing us the present (or past) condition of the world and how to deal with it, much as the gentleman I quoted (paraphrased) earlier mentioned. They almost felt compelled to vote for those books, even while realizing that they might be difficult to read and discuss.

Others looked at the books more on an individual basis and not in a group of three, which was the way I had to look at it in preparation for each quarterly *Happenings* cycle. Of course when they were voting, they had no idea which books would win. Nearly every ballot included at least one work of fiction and one nonfiction book that had nothing to do with war, darkness, or similar themes. Those books just weren't winning in the voting process.

"If we could still read the books we're currently reading with something lighter in between them, I'd be happier," one guy said. That thought simmered in my mind for a long time. Maybe this guy was right; we needed a balance. Maybe that balance would be between fiction and nonfiction or even "dark" nonfiction and nonfiction that was a bit lighter in tone.

After speaking to more and more guys, I decided the best way to make things more agreeable and manageable would be for us to take turns: the guys pick a book, I pick a book, alternating each month. When I presented this to the guys, they all agreed.

For the next *Happenings* cycle I would pick the June and August (2017) books, and they would choose the July title. The voting process was still the same as it had been, only this time they were only voting for one book. (During the next cycle, of course, they would vote for two.) The title they chose would allow me to choose something (for this quarter, two books sandwiching their pick) which was either very different from their book or complementary.

Clearly wanting something lighter (and possibly more related to summertime), the guys chose *Wait Till Next Year*, Doris Kearns Goodwin's memoir of growing up as a Brooklyn Dodgers fan in the 1950s. Surrounding that title, I chose two books that had been nominated by the guys previously. The first was Harper Lee's *To Kill a Mockingbird*, a title that I picked for several reasons. First, I wanted to cleanse the palettes of those who may have read the 2015 Harper Lee novel *Go Set a Watchman*. I didn't (and don't intend to) read that book, but with all the controversy surrounding it, I wanted to revisit Lee's first novel to show that regardless of what comes after it, you can't take away from the beauty and power of *Mockingbird*. Second, I wanted to reread the book myself, since it had been over 20 years since I'd read it and 40 years since I'd read it in high school. I thought other guys would like to reconnect with the book as well.

After *Wait Till Next Year*, I chose *Ender's Game* by Orson Scott Card. This was a book that was nominated on the current ballot by one of our newer members, a book that I had previously not thought of, but thought would be a great pick. I contacted Steve Collier, the guy who'd nominated the book, and asked if it would be okay for me to take it off the nomination list and place on the list as one of my choices, thus making it a sure thing. I told Steve, "It's really your pick and I want you to lead the discussion." He agreed and I believe was rather excited that he wouldn't have to anxiously await the results of the voting process. (Everyone wins!)

I believed that so many of the guys, especially those with military backgrounds, would relate to the book even if they didn't relate to its science fiction elements. *Ender's Game* is nearly always on any list of "Science Fiction for People Who Don't Read Science Fiction," and I think that's probably accurate. It was true in our case: We had a great discussion of the book and Steve did a masterful job of leading it.

The "I pick one, you pick one" process seems to be working well. As of this writing, we continue to use this method with no complaints, at least that I've heard. The guys still have a voice in what gets chosen, which I believe is important, but I also like the fact that I can still pick titles that I think they would enjoy. They still get to choose books they're comfortable reading, and I'm still able to challenge them at times with something different.

Although sometimes members will nominate books that I'm excited about but never get chosen in the voting process. Unfortunately, some good books have slipped through the cracks in this way. Of course I could simply take one of those titles that didn't get enough votes and make it my own choice during the next round, but I'm not sure it would be a good idea to "force" a title on them that they've made clear they don't want to read. I *have*, on a couple of occasions, taken a nomination off the ballot (always with the permission of the guy who nominated it) and chosen it as my pick, all *before* the voting starts (as with *Ender's Game*). Sometimes these were books I was already considering, but in other cases, they weren't.

As the facilitator of the club, one of the greatest compliments I receive occurs when a guy says something like, "That's a book I never would've read on my own, but I'm glad we read it." I sincerely believe the challenge of reading outside of your comfort zone is important, but you probably don't want to do that several times in a row. Have we found a happy medium by alternating their choices and my choices? I think so. This system allows me some much-needed time to discover and evaluate books without the intense time pressure, which (hopefully) leads to better choices and better discussions.

CHAPTER 10

Learning the Guys

When you work in a public library, you soon realize that anyone can come in. That doesn't mean that every person who comes in is necessarily welcome to *stay*. Sometimes we have problem patrons, and yes, sometimes drunk people come into the library.

Most of the people who visit our branch who find themselves in various stages of intoxication are what I'd call quiet drunks. We quickly realize that they're intoxicated, they know it, and they know that *we* know it. They understand we must ask them to leave, and they normally do, usually without fanfare.

I hadn't been working at the library for very long, maybe a year, when we had a drunk guy who wouldn't leave. He was a man in his late 40s, his level of intoxication leaving him still capable of standing up, or in other words, refusing to sit down. Although I was still a fairly new hire, I happened to be the "senior" person at the Info Desk during that particular part of the day (lucky me), sharing the desk with a PTH (part-time hourly staff), thus making me the de facto person-in-charge.

This guy was not only drunk, but also angry about something I couldn't determine. I approached him and tried to be as cool as possible, but nothing I said seemed to calm him down. He was clearly worked up about something, but his mutterings provided no clue. The best idea I could come up with was to steer him as far away from the children's area as possible, but he was having none of it. He began cursing and pulled out a cell phone from his front pants pocket. He slammed the phone down on the floor and stared at me, cursing more. As soon as he reached down to pick up the phone, I instructed one of the circulation staff to call the police.

In my most serene voice, I tried to convince this guy that everything was all right. If I could just engage him in conversation, maybe he would calm down. "Why don't you tell me what's on your mind?" I said. The guy related a story about his daughter who was attending college and apparently no longer wanted him in her life. He began telling me about her, how proud he was of her for going to college, but as he spoke, he grew angry again. He slammed the phone down, picked it up again, slammed it again, picked it up again, all the while extolling his daughter who apparently wanted nothing to do with him. I didn't know what else to do. My intention was to settle him down, to get him thinking about some happier times with his daughter.

"What is she studying?" I asked. He looked confused. "In college," I said. "What's her major?"

His answer was either marine biology or something in a related field. Thankfully he had gone to a happier memory of her, which was exactly what I'd wanted. His voice grew more soothing, gentle. When he ran out of steam, I said, "Tell me more about her."

And he did, but somewhere along the line the anger returned, and he threw the phone down again. I considered grabbing it, but figured that might set him off even further. He didn't seem to want to throw the phone *at* anyone, but was content to pound it onto the carpet. I couldn't be certain if he had anything else in his pockets, but a gun seemed unlikely. Yet it seemed entirely possible he could be carrying a knife.

The man was getting himself worked up again, and I wasn't sure what to do to keep him talking. Then I didn't have to concern myself with it any longer; two policemen walked up and took the guy into custody. Relief flooded over me, thankful that the cops had arrived so quickly since I really had no idea what I would've done next. As I was relaxing somewhat, I noticed two men standing right behind me. I recognized them as guys I'd seen in the library several times before, guys who hung out on the public computers using the internet, guys I'd never spoken to before.

"We had your back," one of them said. "We were ready in case things got ugly." I looked at the other guy and he nodded in agreement.

All this to say that I had a very similar feeling during our discussion of A Walk in the Woods (related in Chapter 8), realizing, perhaps for the first time, that the guys in the book club had my back. More importantly than having my back, they had the best interests of the group at heart. I began reflecting on that night, how a couple of the guys had helped me out of a bad situation by having something ready to contribute when I'd asked for it. Perhaps others were prepared to do the same thing. Without getting too hyperbolic, it was clear that something was developing in the group, something the guys were interested in keeping and protecting. That meant a lot to me then and continues to mean a lot now. I'll never really know, but I often wonder how many guys come to the book club for the books and the discussions and how many come for the company, simply to be around other guys. Perhaps it's a little of both.

Again, not to sound grandiose, but I think the book club offers, in a small way, something that's possibly missing in the lives of these guys. As I often tell people, where else can guys get together other than bars and sporting events and really talk? I can't reasonably think of any other places; maybe you can. I think guys need that. I think *people* need that. We all need a place where we can talk without fear of judgment or ridicule.

Sometimes it seems valuing such a place is one of the things the guys have in common. Although many of these men are in the same basic age range (50-70), you'll find a wide variety of backgrounds. Some are businessmen; others former military. We have one physician, a former attorney, at least four teachers or former teachers, and five published authors. Some have traveled the world. Others rarely leave the Baltimore-Washington area.

Tastes vary as well. One of the guys (who has since moved to another area) came to me after the first meeting he attended, very excited that he'd found a book club. "But look," he warned me, "I'll only come when we're discussing fiction. I don't like nonfiction, don't like it at all." A different guy said the exact opposite thing, that he didn't care for fiction and would come only when we discussed nonfiction works. I suppose those two guys never met...

With some of the guys it took me a long time to learn their likes and dislikes or even if they enjoyed the group at all. One regular attender - I'll call him Leonard - came to the meetings religiously each month, but never said a word. I'd always shake his hand when he arrived, told him I was glad he came, and he always smiled and said, "Thank you," but he never contributed to any of the conversations. I wondered if he was getting anything out of the group.

Then one day a woman came up to the Info Desk and introduced herself as Leonard's wife. "You run the Guys Book Club, is that right?" I told her that I did, and halfway expected her to announce that Leonard wouldn't be coming to any more meetings.

"Let me tell you," she said, "Leonard absolutely *loves* your book group! When he gets home from those meetings it's all he wants to talk about. He comes back and tells me every detail, everything that each guy said about the book. He just won't stop talking about it!"

"I'm so glad to hear it," I told her, attempting to hide my amazement. "You know," I ventured, "Leonard's pretty quiet in the meetings… To tell you the truth, I wasn't exactly sure he was having a good time."

"Oh, he's having a *great* time! He wouldn't miss those meetings for the world!"

You just never know.

Some guys will open up as soon as they walk through the door. Others take a while to warm up, sometimes months. Some have a lot to say. Others, almost nothing. Besides the long-winded guy that attended the discussion of *A Walk in the Woods*, I rarely have to reign anybody in, but it does happen. I try to gently convey the fact that, well, they're talking too much! Invariably those guys will come up to me after the meeting and apologize. One such guy has said to me on at least two occasions, "I know I talk a lot, and sometimes I need to be told to stop." It's almost like I'm a teacher that they feel they must apologize to after class for misbehaving.

The "teacher" aspect of being the group's facilitator also shows up in other ways. Guys will still frequently tell me "I'm really sorry… I've gotta miss the next meeting. We've got a family event" or "I've got to go out of town on business" or some other conflict. It's nice that they tell me these things, and I'm sure most of them do so out of a sense of courtesy. Maybe they also really like the group and don't want me to think they're leaving permanently, but it often strikes me as funny. I've never told them, "Look, I'm not your teacher, I'm not taking roll, you don't have to explain anything to me," but they still do it. Inwardly I laugh, but I do appreciate their intent. (Actually, I *do* take roll.)

As much as I love the group and the guys, there are a couple of things about the club that I wish I could change. First, I wish we could attract more teenagers. We've had some teens join us on occasion (mainly for sports-related books), but usually they don't attend. Those who have joined us are always accompanied their dads. Don't get me wrong, I think that's great. I wish we could have a father/son book club from time to time. Maybe that's something I should try to initiate a couple of times a year. Perhaps that would help get more teens involved.

The second aspect of the group I would like to change is its diversity, or rather, lack of diversity. I love the guys in the book club, but we're almost always a room full of white guys over 50. We've had moments of racial diversity, but they were sadly brief.

One African American man - I'll call him Don - came to at least a couple of our meetings then stopped. At one of the meetings Don attended we were discussing Flannery O'Connor's *A Good Man is Hard to Find and Other Stories*, a collection of Southern short stories sprinkled with characters who often use the "N" word. In the weeks leading up to this discussion, I had warned the guys via email that this book contains language that might be offensive to some readers, and I was hoping that Don had read that email.

As I introduced the book during our meeting, I reiterated that O'Connor's fiction often contains language that may be offensive but that these instances (as far as I can remember) are spoken from the point of view of the author's characters and do not necessarily represent the author herself. I thought that perhaps I didn't need to reiterate that since I'd previously sent the email out, but since Don was present, I decided to bring it up again, stressing that, from what I've read of her, I doubted O'Connor condoned such language herself, and that we at the Guys Book Club certainly don't either.

The subject of racist characters came up a couple of times during the meeting with all the comments handled in a tasteful, respectful manner. If Don was offended by the book or the discussion, he didn't show it. He also didn't come back to the group.

Days passed while I struggled over whether to approach Don. I drafted an email, deleted it, drafted another, then deleted it as well. Maybe I had given enough of a disclaimer, and maybe Don would understand what I had already pointed out. I left it alone, hoping that he might rejoin us in the future. He did not, but I also didn't see him visiting the library, either. Looking back at the situation now, the best thing probably would've been for me to contact him to make sure the book, the group, or the library itself hadn't offended him. But I didn't.

Nearly three years after the meeting for *A Good Man is Hard to Find,* I ran into Don. It was a Saturday and I was screening a double feature of the 1956 and 1978 versions of *Invasion of the Body Snatchers.* During our movies, I normally sit in the back of the room near the entrance. That's where I was when I saw someone open the door and lean in to see what was happening in the darkened meeting room. (This happens frequently.) To my delight, it was Don.

I shook Don's hand and told him how good it was to see him and asked if he'd like to come in and watch the movie. He was dressed in workout clothes and appeared to be either coming from or on his way to the gym, so he declined. He asked how I was doing. "It's so good to see you," I said. "You know, we'd love to have you join us again for the book club." If there was any animosity or ill feelings on his part, I didn't detect it.

"I'd like to do that," he said. "Things have been very busy. We'll see!"

It was wonderful to see Don again, and I was delighted that he hadn't stopped coming to the library. I told him he was welcome at the book club anytime. If the O'Connor book *had* offended him, he seemed to have gotten past it. I'm hoping we will see him again.

Having more diversity in my book selections was also a concern. No one has ever said to me, "You need more diversity in the books you pick," but looking back over the list of books we've read and discussed over the past six years, there have been embarrassingly few ventures into works representing other races, cultures, and lifestyles.

A few of our titles have touched on themes of diversity. For example, Warren St. John's *Outcasts United,* a book about a group of refugee children in Georgia who come together to play on a multiethnic soccer team, and *Hellhound on His Trail: The Stalking of Martin Luther King Jr. and the International Hunt for His Assassin* by Hampton Sides, although that is a book focusing more on the killer than on Dr. King himself. We also discussed Eric Bogosian's *Operation Nemesis: The Assassination Plot that Avenged the Armenian Genocide* and Michael B. Oren's *Power, Faith and*

Fantasy: America in the Middle East: 1776 to the Present, yet both of those books focused primarily on history rather than diversity.

One book zeroed in exclusively on African Americans: *The Golden Thirteen: Recollections of the First Black Naval Officers* (1993) by Paul Stillwell, longtime member of the Guys Book Club (and the same Paul mentioned in Chapter 2). The book included information taken from several interviews by Stillwell with the officers themselves, many of whom were still alive at or near the time of publication. I thought this would be a great book not only for our guys but also to entice African Americans to come to the book club. Since many of the officers chronicled in *The Golden Thirteen* were deceased when we discussed the book in 2015, Stillwell and his writings are a vital (and possibly the only) link to these men, their stories, and their place in American history.

In the weeks leading up to the meeting I spoke to many African American men who came into the library. Although many expressed an interest in attending, none of them showed up.

But many of our regular members did. Twelve guys attended that meeting and were totally engaged, most of them wanting to know more about these men and their amazing lives. All the while I kept wondering how many African American men knew the stories of these naval officers. How many of them had even *heard* of these men? How many recognized the enormous significance not only of the service of these men to our country, but also of their opening the doors to others who would come after them? It would've been great to have African American guys at the meeting.

In early 2019, we read and discussed the novel *Kindred* by African American science fiction author Octavia E. Butler. Once again, no African Americans attended the meeting.

Our lack of diversity was and is discouraging, but I also must realize that the black population in Severna Park is a very low 3.7%[7] Our library has also struggled to bring in more than a handful of attendees for any of our Black History Month programs. It's discouraging to have talented performers such as Kim and Reggie Harris deliver an amazing evening of song to only seven or eight people. One of our best-attended Black History Month programs was a screening of the movie *Selma* (2014), which brought 16 people, only one of which was African American[8].

About a year ago a Latino man in his 30s named Ray attended one of our book club meetings. He contributed to the discussion and seemed to be enjoying himself, bringing some great ideas and points of view to the meeting. A couple of times Ray disagreed with another member's interpretation of a section or passage from the book, but not in an abrasive or intimidating manner. The meeting went well, and I felt that the group was comfortable with Ray and vice versa.

Afterwards I thanked Ray for coming and said we were delighted to have him and hoped we'd see him again. He seemed to have had a good time. I followed up with Ray a few days later via email, reiterating the fact that I was glad he visited the group and hoped we'd see him again, perhaps even as a regular member. He wrote back stating that while he enjoyed the group, he didn't think it was the right fit for him. He didn't go into detail, and I didn't really know whether the group wasn't right for him because of his age (significantly younger

---

7   Severna Park, Maryland (2010), City-Data.com, http://www.city-data.com/city/Severna-Park-Maryland.html

8   Yet perhaps things are changing. We had 34 people in attendance for our 2019 African-American History Month Movie, the documentary *I Am Not Your Negro* (2016), about half of whom were African-Americans.

than most of the guys in the group) or his ethnicity. I told him I respected his wishes to find a better book club fit, recommended Dudes on Books in Howard County, if that wasn't too far a drive for him, and reiterated that he was welcome to come back to the Guys Book Club anytime.

As was the case recently in seeing Don again, I also ran into Ray not long ago. He was waiting to check out some books at the Circulation Desk, and I said hello and told him I was glad to see him. "We'd love to see you at the book club again," I told him. He thanked me and said that he was a little too busy right now keeping up with his children's activities, and I told him I understood.

I often think about why Don and Ray haven't yet returned to the group. Maybe they're simply busy and it has nothing to do with being the only nonwhite people in the room. But maybe they're not comfortable with the group. Putting myself in their shoes, I'd probably be apprehensive at the very least. I'd like to think the guys (including myself) are welcoming. I've never seen any evidence to the contrary. Maybe it's the books we discuss. Maybe it's the demographics of the community. Maybe it's something else entirely, I don't know. But I wish things were different.

I truly believe there's more we need to do as a library and more I can do personally to try to bring more diversity into the branch. I say this not because diversity is a buzzword or because it's trendy to be diverse. I say it because it's important. The library truly is for everyone. We say that all the time, but we really do mean it. Our library is starting to see more diversity with people coming into the building itself, but programming can be a different challenge. But it's one we won't give up on.

CHAPTER 11

Contacting Authors

During the first few years of the Guys Book Club I felt I needed an edge, something that might bring in guys who wanted to come to the group but were reluctant. Maybe I've attended too many author events, but I thought that by having the writer of one of our books show up as a guest, we might attract some guys who were on the fence about attending. But I'll be totally honest: Having an author appearance or two would bring some notoriety to the group.

After the book club had been going for about a year, I began contacting the living authors of the books we were reading. Sometimes finding contact information on writers is difficult, but I usually found what I needed by checking their websites or Facebook pages. In other cases, I contacted the authors' publishers, receiving various responses (that is, when I got back anything at all).

My first response was an email from Malcolm Gladwell's publicist. We had Gladwell's book *Outliers* on the schedule, so I had sent him an invitation through his publisher to attend our discussion of that book. The email was very courteous, thanking me for the invitation, but regretting that Mr. Gladwell's busy schedule would not allow him to attend.

Of course I realized that popular authors such as Gladwell, Michael Lewis *(Moneyball), and* Jim Collins *(Good to Great)* are enormously busy, but I also understood that we live close enough to Washington D.C. and Baltimore that those writers might be in the area from time to time on book tours. It was always a long shot, but it didn't take much time to draft a letter or an email. My biggest surprise was receiving a postcard from Bill Bryson just before our discussion of his book *A Walk in the Woods* (detailed in Chapter 8).

We did have a couple of close calls. Thomas E. Ricks, author of *The Generals: American Military Command from World War II to Today* was interested, but the date we'd chosen for the discussion wouldn't work for him. The same thing happened with Joby Warrrick, *Washington Post* columnist and author of *Black Flags: The Rise of ISIS*, who emailed me that he would love to visit the group, but like Ricks, he had a conflict on the evening of our discussion. Warrick did, however, offer to come another time and talk about the book and his work covering the Middle East in general, which was a nice surprise.

We finally got a solid "yes." Larry Tye, author of *Superman: The High-Flying History of America's Most Enduring Hero* (2012), would be joining us to discuss his book. After a series of emails, Larry graciously agreed to join us, not in person, but via Skype from his home in Boston. Larry confessed that he had never used Skype before, but his kids did, so he had some familiarity with the program.

Several minutes before the meeting, I got our library laptop set up and attempted to contact Larry. After a few false starts, we were finally able to connect with Larry just before the meeting, but with audio only. On Larry's end, he could see and hear us, but couldn't figure out why his video feed wasn't working. As guys gathered in the Conference Room, I tried to talk Larry through what might be the problem with his video feed. Not being a Skype expert, my suggestions were limited. As guys were coming in, a few offered ideas, but nothing we did on our end helped. It seemed there was something on Larry's end that kept his video from coming through. By this time it was probably 7:10 p.m. or so, and I told Larry that we'd be fine with just the audio. He reiterated that we were coming through fine with both video and audio, so we began.

I kicked things off by thanking Larry for joining us and telling him how much we all enjoyed the book. I also mentioned that the guys might have questions as the meeting went on. Larry was a great guest and very informative, answering all my questions about how he came to write the book, what led him to the topic, the writing process itself, and much more. Despite the lack of a video feed, things were going well.

I can't find the attendance record for this meeting (I was so busy with the technology that I probably forgot to record the numbers), but we had at least a dozen guys spread out over a long rectangle of four folding tables. Anticipating this, I had hooked up a pair of small speakers to the laptop in order that everyone in the room could hear Larry. What I didn't anticipate was the problem of having anyone besides me talking to Larry. I sat right in front of the laptop, so it was easy for Larry to hear and see me. But if a guy on the other side of the room had a question, I'd either have to pass the laptop down to him (with the speaker wires attached) or have him step up to the laptop. Too late I realized that either method would've been problematic: the speaker cables only went so far and having the next person ready to address Larry was a real hassle in such a confined space. Passing the laptop around was further complicated by the fact that I'd neglected to charge it ahead of time and was forced to connect it to a power source.

We reached a compromise by placing the laptop at one end of the table so that it could be somewhat moveable and clearing a space at the same end that allowed guys to come up to the laptop to ask their question. This technology snafu on my part undoubtedly kept several guys from asking questions of Larry, but most seemed to be okay with it.

The technology problems certainly kept me from fully enjoying the evening, and I wondered how many of the guys (to say nothing of Larry) felt the same. Larry is far too professional to let a technology problem prevent him from being an effective interviewee, and the guys are too considerate to make their frustrations known, so any disgruntlements or disappointments were not noticeable that night. It was just awkward.

Under the circumstances, the Skype session continued about as well as it could have. After 30 or 40 minutes, I figured we had taken up enough of Larry's time and generosity. I thanked him for joining us and for being so patient with all the technology issues. Larry was, of course, gracious and thanked us for choosing the book and contacting him.

Then an interesting thing happened. As soon as our Skype connection had been broken, it was like someone had given the guys permission to breathe again. I'd been so concerned with the technology issues that I hadn't properly read the guys during the session with Larry. Unsure what had just happened, I simply asked them. "Well, what did you think?"

A couple of the guys looked at one another around the room. I'm not sure who spoke first, but someone said, "I'm glad *that's* over. Now we can say what we really think about the book." Other guys began nodding and I knew I'd completely missed the boat on this.

"It's not that we didn't like the book, or that we don't appreciate the author joining us via Skype," one guy said, "but speaking for myself (and apparently speaking for the majority), I didn't feel like I could be completely honest in front of him."

Other guys chimed in. The consensus was that while most of the guys enjoyed or at least appreciated the book, some found it too long and too detailed. For them, less would've been more. They admired the amount and depth of research Tye had gone to the trouble of compiling and reporting, but they just weren't interested in that much of it. Yet the guys were respectful enough not to be critical in the presence of the author.

Let me be honest: At first that got me steamed. This guy is a professional writer. Authors encounter criticism all the time; they're used to it. Most writers I've met would rather hear an honest criticism than a lot of empty praise. I couldn't understand why some of the guys just didn't say, "Mr. Tye, I enjoyed your book, but why did you feel the need for so much detail?" or "Mr. Tye, great book, but it could've been much shorter." Maybe they thought the venture was simply supposed to be a "feel good" experience in which we only said positive things about the book. Or maybe they saw how much the event meant to me and didn't want to contribute any negativity.

Regardless, I recognized that for the first time at the Guys Book Club, the guys weren't 100% themselves. They held back from giving their most honest, candid opinions, at least while the Skype connection was in place. Once that was severed, it was just like a normal meeting.

That evening taught me that it probably wasn't a good idea to have another guest author visit, so since then, I haven't invited another one to join us.

We *did* have two other authors join us to discuss their books, but these gentlemen were already members of the group. In 2015 we read and discussed Doug Norton's first novel *Code Word Paternity: A Presidential Thriller* and Paul Stillwell's *The Golden Thirteen: Recollections of the First Black Naval Officers.* (I also asked Doug back in 2018 to discuss his second novel, *Code Word: Pandora.*) The atmosphere for these meetings could not have been more different from the Skype session we'd had with Larry Tye. Many of the questions were procedural ones, such as "How did you come up with the idea for the book?" and "What was your process for writing?" All the questions were respectful, yet honest, and I felt the authors answered them both respectfully and honestly, holding nothing back. Rather than a "Let's pat the author on the back for all his hard work," the atmosphere was more "Tell us how you put this thing together and what you were thinking along the way."

During the meeting for Doug's second book, the guys clearly enjoyed the novel, but several readers gave more honest (yet respectful) critical feedback, offering up suggestions for how his next book in the trilogy could be better. I firmly believe their feedback was given in a spirit of helpful criticism, and Doug welcomed these comments and suggestions, taking them graciously.

The guys - and the authors - clearly enjoyed these meetings in a relaxed, open way, something that didn't happen during the Skype session with Larry Tye. Maybe because the guys knew Paul and Doug as members of the book club first and as writers second, it made for more open and honest meetings when we discussed their books. They already knew those guys, and perhaps they felt any criticism would be given with the intent of making future books better. That's the type of situation we could never have with a visiting author, someone none of us had a regular relationship with previously. It's funny: When something doesn't work, everyone knows it. Everyone also knows it when something *does* work.

CHAPTER 12

Women

You may remember from Chapter 1 the discussion I had with my supervisor Heather, who said that if a woman wanted to join the Guys Book Club, I had to let her in. I'd told her at the time that if I did that, it would no longer be a guys book club, defeating the whole purpose. Plus, my branch manager (a woman) had said that I should absolutely *not* allow women into the group. "If anyone has a problem with that," she said, "they can come to me."

From time to time, women would ask if they could attend the Guys Book Club. I politely told them it's a *guys* book club. "But your books are so much more interesting than the books we read in *my* book club," they would say, or "It sounds like your group *really talks* about the book. After five minutes, my group always talks about something else. *Anything* else!" I politely referred them to the listings in *Happenings* of other library book clubs at other branches in the county.

"Well, then," some women would say, "why doesn't the library offer a book club for women?"

We did. Twice during the eleven years I've been at the Severna Park Library (and at least once before I got there in 2008), different librarians have put forth a tremendous amount of effort to develop, organize, and promote an adult book club. For a while, it looked like there was enough interest to sustain one, but after several months the numbers dropped off and it was discontinued.

Why didn't those book clubs work? It had nothing to do with the people running them. In both cases since I've been at the library, the people behind those groups were passionate, dedicated librarians who did everything in their power to make the book club appealing. These clubs featured great books, were carefully planned, and well promoted.

I believe the reason those book clubs didn't work is because our service area already has a large number of private or home-based book groups. I can't tell you how many people come up to the Info Desk on a weekly basis placing holds for books for their book club. Rarely do we have people requesting the same title, so I know there are multiple groups out there. Sometimes I'll ask those patrons (almost always women) "How many people are in your book club?" and numbers range anywhere from four to fifteen or more. I would estimate at least a dozen private book clubs are active in our community alone. With all those book clubs going on, most people are probably reluctant to join another one.

Patrons sometimes ask, "Have you *ever* had a woman attend one of your meetings?" The answer is yes. Several years ago I got a call from one of the librarians at the Crofton branch of AACPL, a library of comparable size to the Severna Park branch. This librarian wanted to start an adult book club at Crofton and wanted to see how one was run. I told her she was more than welcome to visit.

I didn't think any of the guys would freak out, but I told them in advance that we were going to have a guest at next month's meeting, a female guest. A few eyebrows shot up, but most of the guys were intrigued. I explained the situation, that this was another librarian who wanted to start a book club in her branch and would be with us to observe, just as I had done at the Miller Branch of the Howard County system a few years earlier. I assured the raised-eyebrow guys that everything was going to be all right, and it was. At the next meeting the Crofton librarian arrived, we all greeted her with courtesy, and everyone had a great time. Afterward she told me she enjoyed the meeting and came away with lots of ideas for running her own group at the Crofton library.

This happened on two other occasions. Two new hires to our branch also wanted to see how an adult book club was run, so I invited them to come. As in the first meeting with the Crofton librarian, the atmosphere was welcoming and courteous. Again, both librarians expressed having a positive experience, gaining many ideas for their own book clubs should they ever decide to run one themselves.

Three newspaper reporters have asked to visit the group over the years, one of them Sharon Tegler, a woman who writes for *The Capital Gazette* in Annapolis. Everyone enjoyed Sharon's visit, and she wrote a fantastic article on the group, perhaps the best, most accurate representation we've had in print. Sharon still frequents the library and I always enjoy talking with her.

And then we had an incident. Or rather, the guys themselves had an incident. I wasn't even there. Here's what happened:

Due to my wife's work schedule at the time, the only part of the year she had more than a handful of consecutive days off was in mid-July, so that's when we normally took our vacations. 2013 was the first year the Guys Book Club had begun meeting every month *and* the first time we'd met in July. I knew I'd have to miss this meeting and explained the situation to the guys, asking if anyone would be willing to lead that discussion (which happened to be F. Scott Fitzgerald's *The Great Gatsby*). One of the guys offered to lead and I was very grateful, able to enjoy my vacation and relieved that the group wouldn't have to skip a month. Plus I figured it was probably good for the guys to be led by someone other than me from time to time.

When the next year rolled around, I once again needed someone to fill in for me for the month of July. Paul Stillwell graciously offered to lead the discussion of *The Guns of August* by Barbara W. Tuchman. I'll let Paul tell you in his own words what happened next:

> *As I prepared for my role as moderator, I made up a long list of talking points about the book on the beginning of World War I. What I couldn't prepare for was that there would be an additional onslaught besides the one mounted by the Germans in 1914. A woman who had read Tuchman's book had inquired of a librarian whether she could take part, and she was allowed to do so. I wasn't going to exclude her on my own hook. She turned out to be opinionated, not shy about sharing her opinions, and in a number of instances not politically correct. There were three guys in attendance who were new and had not read the book. One was the hatchet woman's husband, who had nothing to contribute. Only one other guy from our regular group was there, and he had read it. As it turned out, he evidently felt uncomfortable with the discussion in progress, because he spent a lot of the time staring at the table in front of him and saying little. It may be*

a coincidence, but I never saw him at one of our meetings after that.

It was a real challenge for me to deal with this often-talking woman and try to draw in the fellow who had read the book. She made a number of broad generalizations that I felt were questionable. I challenged her on one or two but didn't think it was my role as moderator to contradict her. I did pull the discussion back to the topic at hand when she strayed too far off, such as when she said America was headed for doom as the Romans were, and then she started discussing the ancient Romans. A desperate sinking feeling came over me when I looked at the clock at one point and saw that it was 7:20. I thought, "Oh, no, I've got to endure 40 more minutes of this." The one statement that stuck with me came after I tried to evoke some sympathy for the plight of the Belgians, whose country had been overrun by the German Army. Her response: "Screw the Belgians." I felt an enormous sense of relief when the ordeal finally came to an end.

Needless to say, I felt terrible for Paul. I'm not sure who the librarian was who gave this woman the green light to attend the meeting. (No one has ever fessed up to it.) Had she approached me, I would've told her what I tell every woman who wants to visit or join the Guys Book Club:

Normally my first question is "Why do you want to join or visit the group?" Their answer usually tells me a lot. In many cases they're interested only in the particular book we're scheduled to discuss next. These books have no discernible common theme. Titles women have been interested in include the aforementioned *The Guns of August* as well as *Quiet: The Power of Introverts in a World That Can't Stop Talking* by Susan Cain, *The Brilliant Disaster: JFK, Castro, and America's Doomed Invasion of Cuba's Bay of Pigs* by Jim Rasenberger, *The Goldfinch* by Donna Tartt, *Orphan Train* by Christina Baker Kline, *The Boys in the Boat* by Daniel James Brown, and *Ender's Game* by Orson Scott Card, to name a few. (One of our female pages threatened to attend the *Ender's Game* meeting wearing a baseball cap and a fake mustache.) It's hard to predict. Every time I announce a title like *The Nightingale* or *Pride and Prejudice,* I always think we'll have a line of women waiting outside the door for those meetings, demanding entrance (which never happens). It's the ones you *don't* think about, like *The Brilliant Disaster* or *Ender's Game,* that they're interested in.

So again, I'll ask them why they want to visit (or join) the group. Some of them are genuinely dissatisfied with their own book clubs, either with the books that get chosen or the lack of focus. Over and over I hear stories of their book clubs spending five or ten minutes discussing the book and the rest of the time socializing. I sympathize with them and would be dissatisfied as well. In such cases, I'd either try to change things for the better or start seeking out a new book club (which is what they're doing!).

But I believe the real reason why women are disappointed with the Guys Book Club policy is that they feel excluded, as if this group of men is trying to be exclusive.

Well, yes, in a way we are. It's important for men to be able to get together as men and discuss things in a casual, respectful, yet relaxed atmosphere. I always ask these women, "Where else, besides bars and sporting events, can men get together and have meaningful conversations and interactions?" Most women understand where I'm coming from, but not all.

"Well, you could say the same thing about women!" one lady responded.

I don't think so. Women - whether they participate in them or not - often have a greater number of, and different, social outlets generally not open to men. Some of these are moms' groups or organizations focused on children and family concerns. Other groups target issues of particular interest to women only. Maybe some groups have to do with topics that generally don't appeal to men. Or perhaps it has something to do with a void that stems from men not wanting to be joiners. I'm not sure.

It doesn't happen often, but from time to time, some women insist on coming to our meetings. I always tell them, "If you come to the event, no one will prevent you from entering or belittle you in any way. But before attending a meeting, I would ask that you consider the purpose and intent of the group, that this is one of the few outlets these guys have to meet, discuss books, enjoy one another's company, and celebrate reading. I ask that you please respect that." So far, at least, they have.

I've met many of the wives of the guys in the club. Nearly all of them have been supportive of the group and have thanked me for giving their husbands an outlet that allows them to discuss books and be social. (One woman even claimed, in all seriousness, that the book club saved their marriage! I somehow doubt that, but it was nice to hear.) Only one of these women has ever asked me about the policy and she seemed satisfied with my answer.

I did make an exception once. In late 2018, I picked *Bloodsworth: The True Story of the First Death Row Inmate Exonerated by DNA*

Evidence by Tim Junkin. I chose the book for several reasons. First, it sounded interesting. Second, it detailed a Maryland murder investigation, and for the most part, our selections usually don't have a local connection. Third, *Bloodsworth* had been chosen for One Maryland One Book, a program created by a nonprofit organization called Maryland Humanities. One Maryland One Book encourages a diversity of readers from across the state to come together to read and discuss a shared reading experience. Although One Maryland One Book has been around for years, I felt this was the first OMOB title that might really connect with the guys.

I didn't realize that it might also connect with another local book club. In fact, the book was also chosen by an independent book club that was scheduled to meet in our library's conference room (where the Guys Book Club previously met), on the same date, and at the same time we were meeting. What were the chances?

The leader of that group (almost totally consisting of women) emailed me and asked if they could join us for this meeting.

Hmmm… This could possibly set a precedent. But it could also be interesting, maybe even spectacular. Or a complete disaster. How would the guys would react to having another book group joining us? I'd have to think about this.

I trust the advice of my coworkers, so I asked a couple of them how they felt about it. They also thought it *could* be a good idea, but expressed some concerns that it could set a precedent I didn't necessarily want. Yet the potential benefits (to both groups) outweighed the potential negatives. I contacted the leader of the other group and told her that this is an unusual circumstance, but it might be a great opportunity for a one-time get-together. I recommended that each group meet separately for the first half hour, then their club could join us in the larger meeting room to compare notes on the book.

The meeting couldn't have gone better. Both groups were respectful and cordial to the other group and the discussion was open, thoughtful, lively, and enlightening. I'm very glad we did it and I think the guys enjoyed it as well. But I sensed that they weren't interested in doing this on a regular basis. A few of them said as much to me afterward: They were glad we combined for this one book, but didn't want to make a habit of it. If we did, it would no longer be a guys book club. I totally agreed.

I'm not here to start a battle of the sexes, not at all. I have an enormous amount of respect for women. Take a look at my workplace: a public library with (as of this writing) a staff of 17, two of which are men. According to the Bureau of Labor Statistics, 79.5% of library staff in the United States are female.[9] I have good, professional relationships with my female coworkers, and as far as I know, no one has ever accused me of being sexist. I'm not against women; far from it. But I sincerely believe that there's something in our discussions about books that meets a need in these guys' lives. This is not an attempt at grandiosity, but rather an observation. Guys come to the group, and I can actually see them relax, let their collective guard down, and enjoy the freedom to offer their opinions without fear. This doesn't mean that they can't do these things among women. They can. It's just different when it's guys talking to guys. If people think we're sitting around telling inappropriate jokes and trading profanities for an hour, they're wrong. The guys enjoy the

---

9   2016, Bureau of Labor Statistics, http://www.bls.gov/cps/cpsaat37.pdf

book discussions, and I get the impression this group is something they've looked forward to since the last meeting. I know I do.

What many people (including most of my coworkers) don't realize is that our area has *another* men's book club that's been around even longer than ours. Several years ago, one of our regular library patrons noticed one of my posters for the Guys Book Club and came up to the Info Desk and introduced himself. He inquired about the group and said that he'd been a part of a local men's book club for years. We had a great conversation and have shared many titles over the years. (I know of at least one guy who regularly attends both this group and the Guys Book Club. There may be more.)

The difference between this club and the Guys Book Club is that the former does not meet in the library, but rather in men's homes or some other location outside the library. If I'm not mistaken, membership in the group is by invitation only. Yet I wonder how many times women have asked to be a part of this group and what would happen if one (or more) showed up uninvited.

At some point, my branch manager will retire. If I'm still there, the new branch manager may change the policy of the Guys Book Club and open it up to men and women. Obviously it would no longer be the Guys Book Club, but something else. Such a change would not be a tragedy, but it would be at the very least incredibly disappointing. Just getting men to read is hard enough. Removing an outlet where they read, enjoy what they're reading, and delight in discussing what they've read would the reinforce the message that many, many young boys are already getting or have decided for themselves: Reading is not an acceptable activity for guys.

This brings me to one of the primary reasons I started the Guys Book Club: to show boys that reading is not only an acceptable activity, but a fun one, an activity that's also enriching, fulfilling, and, every once in a while, transformative. But that's not the message young guys normally hear.

If you've kept up even casually with reading trends in the U.S., you know that boys have almost always lagged behind girls in reading and reading comprehension. If you don't believe me, you can Google "boys and reading" and sample a few articles and studies. You don't have to read very far to discover that, (1) this problem is not new and (2) it's getting worse.

The Brookings Institution published a report on their website a few years ago titled "Girls, Boys, and Reading" based on the 2015 Brown Center Report on American Education. You can read the entire article (and I encourage you to do so).

https://www.brookings.edu/research/girls-boys-and-reading/

Here are just a few highlights:

Girls score higher than boys on tests of reading ability. They have for a long time. This section of the Brown Center Report assesses where the gender gap stands today and examines trends over the past several decades. The analysis also extends beyond the U.S. and shows that boys' reading achievement lags that of girls in every country in the world on international assessments. The international dimension—recognizing that the U.S. is not alone in this phenomenon—serves as a catalyst to discuss why the gender gap exists and whether it extends into adulthood.

The article goes on to discuss how and why the gender gap happened and continues to occur. Some of this is due to generally slower maturation in boys. Some of it is due to other factors such as socioeconomic conditions. The study seems to focus primarily on how the gender gap affects reading as it relates to test scores, largely dismissing the idea that if boys enjoyed reading more, their test scores could rise. I'm certainly concerned about reading test scores for boys *and* girls, but I'm primarily concerned with developing lifelong readers who read for enjoyment and enrichment.

As a librarian, I've given several presentations on boys and reading, and while I don't have the space to explore all the problems and ideas for solutions here, I will say that one of the major problems I've seen is that many boys feel that reading is primarily a girls' activity. Of course we know that's both a generalization and a ridiculous statement. Reading is for everyone.

Other generalizations also come to mind: Boys generally like pursuits that involve physical activity rather than concentrated nonphysical activities like reading. Boys also tend to read nonfiction rather than fiction and are interested more in learning how things work or other fact-based stories.

Since boys sometimes aren't an easy sell for fiction, any barriers placed in their way make fiction an even greater challenge. As children get older and are handed reading lists from their teachers, those lists are frequently filled with titles like *Little Women, Jane Eyre, The Secret Garden*, and others. Don't get me wrong: I've read them all, and those are great books, but when boys see lists loaded with such books, the message (intentional or not) to them is, "This is not for you."

Again, these are generalizations, but from my experience as a librarian (and including many conversations with teachers over the past 30 years), these can't simply be coincidences.

Also, the challenge of getting any reluctant reader to enjoy reading is made more difficult when the parents don't read themselves. It's like parents telling their children not to smoke when they themselves burn through two packs a day. When parents tell me, "I just can't get them to read," I gently ask how much their kids see *them* reading. A sheepish "not enough" is the response I usually get.

One of the reasons I started the Guys Book Club was to show younger guys that, yes, there *are* grown men who enjoy reading. It's not just one of those adult things that your parents urge you to do when they themselves don't. Not only do we have a Guys Book Club, but these guys *enjoy* talking about what they read. If they weren't having a good time, why would they keep showing up? I want younger guys to look at the Guys Book Club and think, "Wow, these guys are having a great time... And no one's forcing them to read. Maybe they're doing it because they actually like it!"

And they *do* like it. At least so far. Month after month, year after year, they keep coming back for some reason, and I don't think it has anything to do with the popcorn we serve at the meetings. These men enjoy reading and talking to each other about what they read, plain and simple.

Young people - boys and girls - need such reminders, evidence that reading *can* be a lifelong pursuit, and a very enjoyable one. It's ironic that reading - primarily a solitary activity - can also connect you socially with other people who were touched, moved, or even angered by the same book. In a small, but very important way, I think the Guys Book Club is a reminder of all these things.

CHAPTER 13

Problems, Challenges and Mistakes

For a group that's been together for as long as we have (just over ten years as of this writing), the Guys Book Club has experienced very few problems. I'm not even sure "problems" is the correct word; maybe "challenges" would be more accurate. And mistakes? Those were all made by me. (You'll hear about some of them in a moment.)

I think one of the reasons we encounter so few challenges stems from the simple fact that the guys really enjoy reading and discussing books. As pointed out in the previous chapter, although it *is* a guys' book club, we have had women guests from time to time. The women who do visit our meetings usually talk to me afterward, sometimes with a look of astonishment, saying something like "Wow… they really talk about the *book*. For the *entire meeting!*"

Yes, we do. There's usually so much to talk about that the hour sneaks up on us leaving many questions unanswered and topics unexplored. Sometimes we go beyond the one-hour limit. At other times, the discussion continues via email or with several guys hanging around after the official meeting has ended. If the book is good, there's always more to say than we have time to say it.

Yet sometimes people feel they must share *everything* about a book in one breath. While it hasn't happened often, we have had some long-winded people attend our meetings. Usually these are well-intentioned guys who like to comment on certain books and just don't know when to stop. (I've only had to stop guys a handful of times, the worst of which I described in Chapter 8.)

Other guys just get a bit carried away, usually because they have a strong knowledge of or connection to the subject matter. We've had engineers talk in detail about the engine design of the Wright Brothers' airplanes in David McCullough's book, as well as a rower describing and validating what Daniel James Brown wrote about in *The Boys in the Boat*. Veterans have told of their experiences, comparing them to several books we've read. To my knowledge, we've never had a guy at the book club who worked for the FBI or CIA, but if they did, they couldn't talk about it anyway, so who knows?

These guys bring such a wide variety of work and life experience to the group that there's almost always some connection to whatever book we're reading. Sometimes that connection is simply a passion for a book, its author, or the genre. When we were preparing to discuss a collection of Edgar Allan Poe stories for October 2013, one member asked if he could read Poe's famous poem "The Raven" to the group. I thought it was a good idea, but didn't realize that he was going to *perform* the poem (with a stuffed, yet lifelike raven as a prop) from memory. It was an amazing moment.

Other guys have brought in additional books, newspaper clippings, and other items to complement the works we're discussing, sort of a grown-up version of Show-and-Tell. One member brought in a replica of a tugboat for a discussion of Michael J. Tougias and

Casey Sherman's *The Finest Hours*. Others have brought in personal memorabilia connected to the books we've read. This is always wonderful to see, knowing that these guys are not only enjoying the books, but often making a personal connection to these works that can't help but build even more enthusiasm among everyone.

These are pleasant surprises rather than problems or challenges. As you read in the early chapters of this book, most of the difficulties occurred in getting the club off the ground. After that, I just had to avoid making mistakes that could hinder the group. Although I've made many more than this, I'd like to talk about three specific mistakes I made with the Guys Book Club, two of them relatively small (mistakes that I've already shared with the group), one large (that I haven't shared until now).

One small mistake (again, publicly acknowledged by me) occurred in June 2018. Months before, knowing that it was my turn to pick the June book, I was talking to my coworker Samantha Zline. She was reading *Mindhunter: Inside the FBI's Elite Serial Crime Unit* by John E. Douglas and Mark Olshaker. The title is a reissue of the original 1995 book, republished to coincide with the release of the Netflix original series *Mindhunter*. As Sam was reading it, she began telling me how gripping the book was and how much she was looking forward to the Netflix series based on it. I noticed the book title and immediately thought, "I've read this! It was a long time ago, but I read it." I remembered it as a compelling page-turner, one that dropped you into the real-life stories of Douglas and the rest of his FBI colleagues in tracking down serial killers. Since I already had several other titles I was considering for the group, I didn't immediately pick up *Mindhunter* for another read.

Instead, I watched the Netflix series and was blown away by the difficulties Douglas (renamed Holden Ford for the show) encountered in gaining acceptance and approval for the serial crime unit. Douglas's idea was that in order to catch these killers, you have to know what they know and think like they think. The only way to accomplish that was to talk to them, the ones who were safely behind bars. From there, FBI serial crime unit professionals could gather and examine data, formulating profiles of current killers still at large, which would hopefully lead to arrests and convictions.

That process is no easy task, and the Netflix series does a masterful job of portraying those challenges. After watching the series, I thought, "Wow, I know it's been over 20 years since I read the book, but I really don't remember much of this…" I started rereading the book. I'd only gotten through the introduction when it was time to send in our book titles for the next round of *Happenings*, so I included *Mindhunter* as my June pick. Several other things kept me busy during that time, so I didn't get back to the book for several weeks. When I did, after reading 50 or so pages, I realized, "I've actually never read this book!"

I had mistaken *Mindhunter* for another Douglas book I *had* read, *Journey Into Darkness*. In *Journey Into Darkness* (published two years after *Mindhunter*), Douglas continues to describe more cases using behavioral profiling and investigative analysis, making it something of a continuation of *Mindhunter*. As I was preparing for our meeting by reading and taking notes on *Mindhunter*, I realized that the Netflix series - even though possibly containing fictionalized elements - was far superior to the book in several ways.

In the series, FBI Agent Holden Ford (Jonathan Groff), a stand-in for Douglas, combines traditional crime-solving techniques with psychology and sociology, something quite foreign to the Bureau at the time. Ford and his partner Bill Trench (Holt McCallany) struggle at first to get the program recognized and approved from the Bureau's higher-ups, fighting enormous skepticism and bureaucracy. Even when things start rolling, Ford - after interviewing a few serial killers face to face - realizes he has perhaps made a fatal mistake in under-preparing for these encounters. As Ford and Trench seek to compile psychological profiles of deadly killers, they run into resistance from various other law enforcement agencies, the very people they're trying to help.

The combination of breaking unexplored territory in crime solving, fighting the very agency you work for, keeping some semblance of a normal life, and avoiding death at the hands of serial killers makes for a tension-filled television show. Unfortunately much of that is absent from the book. Don't get me wrong: *Mindhunter* contains some incredible stories and is often riveting, but the work frequently comes across as an opportunity for John Douglas to spotlight John Douglas. Make no mistake, Douglas and his efforts should be celebrated. He has been responsible for many of the innovations and improvements in helping to understand and capture serial criminals. But he also blows his own horn. A lot. That turned me off, and I feared it would turn off the guys as well.

So here I was, preparing for a meeting on a book I thought I'd read and hadn't, plus it was a book I wasn't very enthusiastic about. I didn't want to wreck the discussion for the guys, so I didn't mention my mistake until everyone had given his general opinion about the book. Then I told them I'd chosen the wrong book and apologized. They were all fine with it and at least a few of them shared the same misgivings I'd had about the book. No harm, no foul, but I was still embarrassed.

Another mistake is one that happens largely due to the amount of time between reading and choosing a book. I'll often read a book that I'm very excited about, thinking, "Wow, the guys are going to *love* this one!" and add it to my list of books to select when it's my turn to pick. From time to time, I'll revisit such a book in preparation for our meeting, only to realize it wasn't such a great choice.

This happened with *I'll Be Gone in the Dark: One Woman's Obsessive Search for the Golden State Killer* (2018) by Michelle McNamara. I finished the book in September 2018 and enthusiastically chose the title for our March 2019 meeting. The problem in picking books so far in advance is that, (1) your enthusiasm for the book might wane and (2) you realize that maybe the book was a good fit for the group *when you read it*, but not necessarily for the date you scheduled it. That's exactly what happened with *I'll Be Gone in the Dark*.

In reading the book a second time, I couldn't reconnect with the story or get very excited about it. Perhaps this is because the book is so disturbing or because the work had to be finished by others when McNamara died. It also felt a bit anticlimactic now that the Golden State Killer has (with a high degree of certainty) been captured. Regardless, I wasn't looking forward to discussing the book.

The night of our meeting, I wasn't surprised to find that most of the guys didn't care for the book. While it's still a good read, I couldn't generate much enthusiasm for it the second time around. I mentioned my misgivings to the guys, telling them that occasionally I'll read a book, get excited about it, choose it for the group, then, during preparations for the group, discover that perhaps it wasn't a great pick. They seemed to understand. Will it happen again? Possibly, but I hope not.

The larger mistake, up until now, has been known by only two people: myself and a book club member (and friend) named Jim Haas.

Ever since the guys started nominating books for our group, I'd look over those nominations with a mixture of delight, surprise, indifference, and in some cases, dread. There have been times when certain titles and/or authors have been nominated, books and authors I don't really care for. Sometimes such titles and authors have won enough votes to be selected and we read them, despite my personal feelings about those works and writers. At times, I discover that the book/author I was dreading really wasn't so bad. In other cases, the experience is as painful (or more so) than I had anticipated. But those instances are few.

I rarely watch television anymore, but years ago I'd sometimes catch *The O'Reilly Factor* with political commentator Bill O'Reilly. I saw a few of these shows, perhaps because I was interested in O'Reilly's guest for a particular episode, or maybe because the show was what happened to be on. It didn't take long before I realized that O'Reilly's guests were not there for a conversation, at least not a civil one. O'Reilly frequently interrupted his visitors, giving his own thoughts and opinions before they could finish theirs. I usually didn't agree with his views and even in the rare instances when I did, I found his manner rude and bullying. In short, he offended me. (To be fair, O'Reilly is far from the only television, radio, or podcast host who utilizes this method. He was simply the first I had encountered.)

O'Reilly began writing and co-writing books back in 1998, but his "Killing" series premiered in 2011 with *Killing Lincoln: The Shocking Assassination that Changed America Forever*. The series has continued with several other "killing" books focused on the actual chronicles of famous historical figures as well as their deaths. Other books feature the killing of John F. Kennedy, Ronald Reagan, General George Patton, Jesus, and more.

O'Reilly authors these books with Martin Dugard, a man who's been writing professionally since 1988. O'Reilly has been a journalist for many years, so it's not clear how the writing of the "killing" books is divvied up. I'm also not sure how the research is conducted or cited.

The O'Reilly books began showing up on Guys Book Club nomination lists several years ago, and early on they received a fair number of votes, but never enough to win the ballot. Although I'd never read any of them, and despite my dislike for O'Reilly, I wondered why anyone would read them since you could find plenty of books written on Kennedy, Reagan, Patton, etc., by people who knew their subjects, books from qualified scholars and experts that had stood the test of time and were recognized as legitimate works. Of course I soon realized the selling point was O'Reilly himself. It didn't matter what or who the subject was. His audience was so large that anything with the O'Reilly stamp on it was going to sell.

Then, prior to one nomination cycle, Jim Haas told me that he'd read one of the O'Reilly books and really enjoyed it. I was stunned. Jim is a fine writer and has authored several works of nonfiction on a variety of subjects, and I know firsthand that he does exceptional research. For many years, I, along with several of my coworkers, have helped Jim acquire several books and articles for his research through interlibrary loan, so I knew he understood the value of good research. But it amazed me how much he liked an O'Reilly book. A conversation ensued. (Some of this was face to face, but much of our correspondence in this matter was via email.)

"Have you read any of these O'Reilly books?" Jim asked.

"No," I replied, "and I won't."

"Why not?" Jim asked.

"I've seen O'Reilly's television show and find the man offensive," I stated.

Our conversation continued and I sensed Jim was losing patience with me. He asked what I would do if one of O'Reilly's books were chosen for the book club. I told him that I'd read it, but that I would not lead the discussion. Now Jim was stunned.

Jim was clearly upset with me and I didn't understand why, at least not immediately. We didn't speak or email for several days, perhaps weeks. I was concerned that I had lost Jim as a member of the book club and, more importantly, as a friend.

I began to examine what I knew and what I didn't know. On a personal level, O'Reilly was offensive to me. Based on what I saw on the show, the man portrayed himself as a rude bully. I didn't want to have anything to do with him or his work, even if that included books that were probably researched and ghostwritten by someone else.

But I also knew that I've enjoyed quite a bit of work from other people who were equally offensive to me: composers, singers, actors, filmmakers, etc. You read and hear a lot these days about separating the artist from the art, "Judge the work, not the jerk," and while everyone is going to have a different opinion about where they fall in that argument, it's a discussion that's probably never going to go away.

What I *didn't* know was what the O'Reilly books were like. I had no idea. Was it unfair for me to judge those books without having read any of them? Yes. I wasn't giving the man a chance. Even further, I wasn't practicing what I preach. Librarians frequently advise patrons to read widely, even (maybe *especially*) authors they may not agree with. I wasn't doing that. Further still, by telling Jim that if one of those books were chosen, I would refuse to lead the discussion, I was essentially telling the guys, "I won't lower myself to leading a discussion on this book, but if one of *you* wants to do that, fine."

How arrogant and insulting. It was almost as if I were behaving to the book club the same way O'Reilly did on his show. It now became clear how my attitude and comments were so offensive to Jim. I approached Jim and apologized, and he graciously accepted my apology. Although this was a private incident, I wanted to discuss it here (and with Jim's permission) to show that I still have a lot to learn.

Although they continue to be published, only one O'Reilly book has been nominated since his departure from Fox News in 2017. It didn't win, but it got a fair number of votes. Although my opinion of O'Reilly hasn't changed, if one of his books wins, I'll read it and lead the discussion (unless the person who nominated wants to lead; that's how it works, as spelled out in Chapter 9). If I can ask other readers to read books or authors they don't like (which I'm sure has happened many times), then I should be expected to do so. I might even learn something about myself.

When I was a band director and had the opportunity to mentor student teachers or new teachers, I would usually tell them, "You'll learn more from the students than they'll learn from you, at least in the beginning, and that's okay. Embrace it." It's not just at the beginning of the teaching/facilitating process that this holds true. It happens all the time. I'm very fortunate to be surrounded by a group of guys who are gracious enough to be so forgiving.

CHAPTER 14

It's Not About Me

As soon as the group began voting on the books we'd discuss, I thought it would be a good idea to have the person who nominated the winning book lead that title's discussion. Sure, this decision was a little selfish on my part. Having someone else leading the group would take the burden off me for a month, and with my recently added duties as a Librarian 1, any timesaver was welcome. If the guy who nominated the book was passionate about it, his facilitating of the discussion would likely add more interest to it than would mine. More importantly, this decision allowed the opportunity for some of the other guys to lead from time to time.

The guy whose book is chosen gets the first right of refusal. He can lead the discussion for that meeting or he can decline, in which case I will facilitate. Only on a few occasions has anyone turned me down. It seems anytime you get to talk about something you're passionate about, the chances are good that passion will become contagious to the rest of the group. I've seen guys whom I'd previously thought shy and reserved come wonderfully alive leading these events. One man who almost never contributed to previous meetings delivered one of our finest discussions. I'm convinced that some of these guys are just waiting for an opportunity to share their knowledge about a book, its subject, and/or its author.

But those who lead these meetings learn a lot as well. Frequently a week or two before the event, the leader of that book's discussion will contact me and ask, "How should I run the discussion? What should I do first? What should I do after that?" and other questions.

I tell them to do what feels natural. Talk to us like you're talking to a friend over a cup of coffee. Don't feel you must imitate me or my format. Some do that anyway, maybe because they don't want the format to change even though the person leading the group has changed. I understand that, but what I do works for me and seems to work for the group. When you vary the facilitators, you're inviting the possibility of changing the direction and tone of the discussion, something many of the guys no doubt welcome. Plus, I'm sure the guys get tired of listening to me every month. (I know I would, and frequently do!)

Everyone who's ever led the group has been well prepared. Many come with extensive, detailed notes, some with a brief outline, others with nothing (which doesn't mean they're not prepared). One of the best of these facilitators has been Paul Stillwell. I've watched him lead several discussions, and he does a professional job of asking questions from his notes, yet is able to read the group as the meeting progresses, knowing when to let them carry the discussion organically and when to reign it in when they start to drift off topic. It probably helps that Paul is a fine writer and a captivating speaker, but he seems to know intuitively how to keep things moving in an interesting way.

Steve Collier led a great discussion of Michael Ondaatje's novel *Warlight*, a challenging novel several of the guys initially didn't care for very much. Steve did a first-rate job of gently (and strategically) asking questions that touched on specifics about the book, working with the tenacity of a professional interrogator, but also with the quiet gentleness of a caring instructor. I think Steve's approach of modifying a facilitating method they were familiar with by unobtrusively challenging the guys to rethink various aspects of the book was simply masterful.

Although I no longer use this method, at the time I would kick off meetings by having the guys go around the table one at a time, giving the book a rating from 1 to 10, followed by a few brief thoughts. Steve built on this by asking several *specific* questions about the novel using the same method. You could almost see the guys sweating, knowing that their turn was coming, and they had to have an answer to a specific question, making them attempt to put their finger on *exactly* what they thought about specific aspects of the novel. I doubt this would've turned into a "I just didn't like the book" gripe session, but Steve's handling of the meeting guaranteed such an occurrence would not happen.

Many other guys have done excellent jobs facilitating as well. Our group is blessed to have a wealth of men who aren't afraid to lead and put themselves out there. It makes a huge difference when a guy like Nino Martini, who spent time as a seaman, leads the discussion on *The Finest Hours* by Michael J. Tougias and Casey Sherman, or when Bill Saur, who lived and worked in Sarajevo, led us through Steven Galloway's *The Cellist of Sarajevo*.

Part of this cross-section of experiences no doubt comes from the fact that we live so close to Washington D.C., which means the number of people with military, political, and other government backgrounds will be significant. (This may also account for the group's eagerness to choose and discuss historical and military works.) This does not surprise me.

What does surprise me is the fact that so many of the guys in the group tend to frequently agree on so many issues. Sure, we have our disagreements, and while they may grow in intensity, I have never witnessed anyone behave in a manner you could call arrogant or rude. I've never had to act as a referee or a peacemaker, at least not seriously. Maybe this has something to do with people who read widely, people willing to objectively consider points of view other than their own.

Don't get me wrong: members have disagreed wildly over the worth of a book or a writer. At one of our recent meetings, one of the guys commented about that night's selection, "I think this book sucks." No one at the table burst in with a "Hey, wait a minute, pal…" or "Oh yeah? Well maybe *you* suck!" or any other retaliatory rejoinder. This guy was allowed to state his opinion freely, which is what the book club is all about.

Now that doesn't mean this guy's comment went unchallenged. Others around the table, rather than saying, "You're wrong; let me tell you why," instead spoke of the book's strengths and aspects they appreciated.

Voicing a negative opinion in a meeting when none have been previously expressed can open the floodgates for everyone to engage in some serious book-bashing. If it's a book most guys don't like, all it takes is one person to create a crack in the retaining wall. That usually doesn't happen, but when it does, I try to quickly assess the situation and ask myself, "Are they ranting, or is this particular complaint about the book legitimate?"

What usually happens in those cases is that some of the guys will gently ask probing questions to find out what specific part of the book/idea/philosophy the person in question has an issue with. Most of these guys are asking such questions not so much as challenges, but rather as points of clarity so we can all understand where this reader is coming from. Although we've never had heated arguments, we have certainly experienced disagreements. Again, these have always been civil, at least according to what I've seen *in the room*. What happens beyond the library doors is anyone's guess.

Although these last few paragraphs seem like a digression, I really do have a point or two in writing them. First, differences of opinion are going to happen, I don't care if there are only two people in the room. You're going to get to a point where one person disagrees with the other. The more people you add to the mix, the greater the likelihood that disagreements will occur. It's how the group handles those disagreements, and particularly how the facilitator handles them, that's important.

Second, some of the guest facilitators have asked me about leading other groups outside of our library's service area. One group member, Don, told me that he and his wife would soon be moving out of state, and that while their new community has a wonderful library, they don't have a book club for guys. He wanted to start one. I was, of course, delighted to hear this for many reasons (one of which I will discuss at length in the final chapter). Since Don started attending the Guys Book Club a few years after we'd started, I told him about the early days, how things got started, my approach, and all the rest. I also told him, "This isn't the only way to do it; it's just how I did it here. I can tell you more about how *not* to put a book club together rather than how to do it."

That is one of the purposes of this book: to help equip anyone, male or female, to organize and lead a book discussion group. I hope that what I've shared with Don personally and in this book will be helpful for him and anyone else thinking about launching a book club. Again, this is just one guy's experience, and every situation/library/community is different. What works at the Severna Park Library might not work the same where you are. But the ingredients are the same everywhere: people who are passionate about reading good books and are willing to discuss them in an open, welcoming, non-judgmental environment. Again, I'll discuss the importance and need for such groups in the last chapter, but we have one more topic to cover before we get there...

CHAPTER 15

Discussing Books Nobody Liked

Sometimes you realize, too late, that you've chosen the wrong book. As the leader of a book discussion group, you're often choosing which books the club will read and discuss based on what you think they'll like. You understand that everyone won't like every book, but when you come to the awful realization that possibly *no one* will like the book you chose five months ago, and it's too late to change it, it's not a good feeling.

I've already described the groups' nearly unanimous dislike of Cormac McCarthy's *No Country for Old Men*, but there were a couple of other instances when a sizable percentage of the guys did not like a particular book. Yet the minority will often be vocal in their defense of such books, keeping me from having to do all the heavy lifting. But not always. I'm the one responsible for choosing the book, and it's my responsibility, perhaps not to defend it, but to justify my reasons for choosing it. "Because I like it" is not a good enough reason to choose a title, although I'll admit I've done that.

Rather than defending my position, I try to defend the book. I will tell them what I saw in the work that made me choose it, something that I thought they would appreciate or relate to in some way.

I didn't know if *Transit* by Anna Seghers would work, but I knew that the guys enjoyed books (fiction or nonfiction) on World War II. It also helped that some of them knew enough about refugees and such matters as obtaining letters of transit during an occupation, ration tickets, and similar wartime challenges. I had hoped that these familiar aspects would be enough to draw them into the nightmarish, almost Kafka-like world of *Transit*. I think that for the most part, while they may not have embraced the book, most of them at least appreciated it. When I touched on those aspects of the Seghers novel, they were more willing to give it further consideration.

Recently I chose Ray Bradbury's *Something Wicked This Way Comes*, a novel I had first read as a teenager, then as a middle-aged adult about ten years ago. As a teen, I felt carried away both by the atmosphere and the story, but when I revisited it decades later, I was surprised by Bradbury's poetic language. I had a hard time coming to grips with the novel, feeling that the language took me out of the story, but I still enjoyed it.

When I chose the book for the group, I hadn't revisited it in a decade. Rereading it I soon thought, "Oh boy, they're gonna hate Bradbury's flowery language here. I'd better prepare myself for the worst."

I came up with talking points such as "Bradbury is writing in the voice of the boys here. It's not meant to reflect reality but fantasy, the wonder and possible danger involved in carnivals," and such. I was also prepared to talk about how I viewed the book as a young person decades ago, identifying with Will and Jim, the novel's young protagonists. I was about their age and shared their same dreams, hopes, and fears. I'm now older than the character of Will's dad Charles

Holloway and understand his fears of becoming an elderly man, approaching old age and death. The book hadn't changed; I had.

There's a conscious thought process that lies behind every book I choose, some reason I decided to pick this book and not that one. Whether I realize it at the time or not, each book contains something I think is worth communicating to the group. It may be an idea, a theme, a character, a philosophy, or even a feeling. Sometimes the journey to those concepts becomes more difficult when the book's "packaging" doesn't initially go down easily. Anything that can potentially get in the way, such as Bradbury's poetic language in *Something Wicked This Way Comes*, must be addressed. That may make a difference, or it may not, but it should be addressed.

Of course you want everyone to enjoy every book, but if you're reading a variety of works, that's not going to happen, and really, it *shouldn't* happen. I sometimes want to challenge my readers, make them look at the world from a different vantage point, consider someone else's life, race, country, philosophy, or worldview. Reading the same type of book gets boring very quickly. You don't want to turn around one day and suddenly wonder where everyone in your book group went.

For years I've thought about having the group read *A Clockwork Orange* by Anthony Burgess, but I know my guys, and I don't think some of them would have the patience to get through the novel's amazingly inventive slang. Maybe I'll change my mind on that some-day, but I think the rewards, at least for right now, may not be worth the effort. *Right now.* You must choose your battles.

So if you lead a book club, I challenge you to mix it up from time to time. Sure, give them what they want, but also present them with books that will cause them to think differently. Don't set out to offend your readers or give them too much of a challenge too soon, but do stir things up a bit.

CHAPTER 16

Saying Goodbye

One of the hardest parts of leading a book club for a long time is watching members leave. I've been greatly saddened to have lost several great guys who have relocated to different areas over the years. Usually those moves are necessitated by job transfers, wanting to be nearer to children or grandchildren, or retirement. It's a real honor when those guys tell me, "Please keep me on the email list!" I'm delighted they want to stay in touch with the group and remain connected with what's going on.

Some of these guys who've relocated contact me from time to time, others on a more frequent basis. One member who relocated to Washington D.C. drops into the library occasionally. It's always a pleasure to hear from him, and he still reads many of the books on our list. (He even "votes" from time to time for upcoming titles, although he realizes I can't legitimately count his votes… Unless he comes back to join us!)

In the previous chapter I mentioned Don, who will be moving to Florida soon and wants to start his own book club once he gets settled there. When Don told me this months ago, I was astounded and overjoyed that he also has a passion for getting guys to read and discuss books. I wish him all the best and hope he won't be the last guy in the group to try to establish a book club for guys in other areas. (Maybe someone reading this book will consider it. I hope so.)

Saying goodbye to these guys isn't easy, but it doesn't compare to the difficulty of losing someone permanently. When a member of the Guys Book Club passes away, we're all affected. That's happened at least twice.

In one case, the widow of one of our members named Fred, contacted me to ask me to please not send any further emails since her husband had recently passed away. Although Fred had only attended sporadically, I remembered him as a warm, personable guy whom everyone enjoyed. Later some of the other guys who'd gotten to know him better talked about the conversations they'd had with him and how he always had such a wonderful, friendly demeanor.

Another widow came up to the Info Desk to tell me that her husband had passed away and mentioned how much he enjoyed the club. Dick was a gentleman who'd been a faithful member of the Guys Book Club for years, always asking about upcoming books, commenting on the ones he liked (which were most of them), and telling me how much he enjoyed the group and our discussions. It was always a pleasure to see him. Dick was a passionate reader, and although not the most talkative guy in the group, he was always very conversational with me and the other members.

While Fred's passing was sudden, Dick's was more drawn-out. Both were difficult for me and the rest of the guys to accept. Dick had clearly been slowing down the last few times I'd seen him, walking a bit more carefully, taking additional effort in getting around the library. When his wife told me he'd passed away, I tried to remember the last time I'd seen him at a meeting, realizing it had probably been several months. Then I began thinking about other guys I hadn't seen in a long time. We've always had several members in their 70s and some in their 80s, and when someone in that age range has been absent for a few meetings, you begin to wonder if everything's okay.

It dawned on me that I should probably start contacting some of those guys to make sure they're all right. I'd admit it: I always breathe a sigh of relief when one of the guys I haven't seen in a while walks into the library. I always greet them and tell them that we've missed having them at the meetings. Their usual response is something like, "Well, we were out of town" or "I was really sick for a while," or something to that effect. Whatever the response, it's always good to see them.

Yet I realize that time moves on. People are going to leave the group for various reasons including, let's face it, death. This was something I never thought about when I started the Guys Book Club, how to deal with the passing of one or more of its members. Maybe I never expected the book club to go on as long as it has. As a band director, I was used to seeing the same kids for three or four years, after which time they moved on to the next level of their educational journey. The situation with the book club is certainly different, but I've seen some of these guys for ten years. You get to know people in that amount of time, get used to having them around, and when they're suddenly gone, you find yourself a little unsteady (or at least I do). I correspond with several of these men on a regular basis and have enjoyed spending time with some of them outside the book club. In many cases, these correspondences and meetings have little or nothing to do with the book club. I simply enjoy hanging out with them on an individual basis, something you rarely get to do with the group (unless they arrive early or stay late).

But it's the group atmosphere that I cherish most, having several guys gathered around a table, sharing their thoughts about books. You get used to them and enjoy learning their mannerisms, quirks, ways of thinking, and various personalities. There are quiet ones who don't say much, but you can see the enjoyment in their eyes. There are others who always have something light and humorous to add when we're discussing a book that might be a little too dark or heavy. Others share how a particular book affected them, holding nothing back. Many bring a whole new dimension to our discussions with their rich and varied life experiences. Some don't seem to like anything we read and others love just about every book. There's a great deal of comfort in being with these guys, and when we lose one of them, part of that comfort is gone.

But isn't that the way life is? We all meet people, get to know them, and establish relationships, knowing full well that these bonds aren't permanent. As they say, there are only two certainties in life: We grudgingly face one each April and do everything we can to avoid the other. I don't mean to sound like one of those *Chicken Soup for the Soul* books (may one *never* be chosen for the Guys Book Club), but maybe that makes us more thankful and appreciative of the relationships we *do* enjoy, even those forged in a book club with a bunch of guys.

I'm probably too close to it. You should talk to the guys and let them tell you their stories.

I'll close this chapter with a story that initially gave me a quick chuckle, then became something I've never forgotten. A couple of years into the book club, my manager Karen asked how the group was going. I told her it was going very well, but lately I was feeling like a teacher again.

"How do you mean?" she said.

"Well, you know I've always sent out email reminders to the guys before our next meetings, but lately some of the guys send back replies saying they're sorry they can't come due to some conflict or another, but *promise* they'll make it for the next one. It's like I'm a teacher taking roll and they're afraid they're going to get in trouble for skipping class!"

"That's not it at all," Karen said.

"Why else would they do it, then?" I asked.

"Because they care," she said.

CHAPTER 17

Moving Forward

I t seems fairly obvious: People who belong to book clubs usually like to read books. It *seems* obvious, but from what I've heard from other people, book clubs are often an excuse for social get-togethers. Fine, call it a social get-together, then, or whatever you want to call it, but don't call it a book club unless you're talking primarily about books. Again, I've been very fortunate to be the leader of a wonderful group of guys who truly love reading and discussing books, but I'm not responsible for their love of reading. Maybe (in a very small way) I helped develop that love of reading, but I didn't get it started. Someone else did.

Our library system spends a lot of time and effort in developing and encouraging early literacy. That involves school and preschool outreach visits, community events, and especially early literacy programs such as Babies in Bloom, Toddler Time, and Preschool Storytime. Every library in our system offers these programs, usually once a week or more. These programs are suited to the needs and abilities of the children they target. With babies, you read to them (usually with a board book), recite rhymes, sing songs, and more, all of which introduces and reinforces language, preparing their young minds to embrace and become familiar with words and sounds.

With toddlers, you can read actual picture books that further explore sounds, letters, words, rhymes, songs, and more. In Preschool Storytime, the books are more challenging, more sophisticated, and you can focus on concepts and help develop skills that will make them better prepared to read. If all of this sounds too academic and boring, it's not. At least not at my branch.

Each presenter in each library does things a little differently, and every staff member brings his or her strengths to each program. My wife and I do not have children, and I'm the youngest in my family, so I have practically no experience with babies, yet I've presented Babies in Bloom programs for thirteen years. I enjoy them, but I'll be honest: I always wonder if my babies programs are effective. Babies typically can't respond in a way that shows they've got it and are on the right track. I know, however, that my coworkers and I are laying the groundwork here, and we're just enforcing (hopefully) what the babies' moms, dads, and sometimes grandparents are doing at home.

With the toddlers and preschool kids, it's different. They're old enough to watch and listen to everything you do and respond. I almost always open those programs with a song by Raffi called "Shake Your Sillies Out," which (I hope) conveys to the kids that what we're about to do in Storytime is unapologetically fun. When I read a story, I try to choose books that allow them to respond or participate in some way. Maybe there's a word or phrase I'll ask them to shout out when we get to it in the book, or maybe it's just asking questions as we read. ("Look at that tiger! What do you think he's going to do?") It's an interactive experience. They're not just being read to, they are *actively* participating in the story.

Although it's much too early to tell them this, I'm trying to convey the idea that reading is an interaction between the reader and the author. It's like the writer is making a contract with the reader: "I'll write a story, but you have to bring something to it as well." That something is experience, background, curiosity, a desire to know more, a questioning (even skeptical) nature, and an attitude of "Show me something I haven't seen before." We don't want the listeners just sitting there waiting for something to happen to them. We want them engaged in the story.

That type of engagement is what I seek to maintain and develop over the lifetime of the reader, through grade school, middle school, high school, college, and beyond. Along the way on that journey, however, are many opportunities to snuff out that engagement and love of reading. I've seen it happen both as a teacher and as a librarian, and I don't like it. In fact, I despise it. Engagement should not diminish, but rather grow over the years, all the way to the end of our reading lives. That may be the most exciting aspect of the Guys Book Club: These guys, some of them in their 80s, are still engaged with reading. Again, I didn't have anything to do with that initial engagement, but in a small way, my coworkers and I are a part of helping younger (and perhaps older) readers develop and maintain it.

My concern is that we - a society, a culture, a nation - are not actively furthering this engagement. (I'll most likely step on some toes here, but I care more about the importance of reading than shielding someone's feelings, so there we have it.) We bring children to the library to attend early literacy programs and check out books, and that's wonderful. I'm always glad to see that. But do our children see *us* reading regularly? Do we, as adults, talk to each other about what we're reading?

When I was growing up, both of my parents smoked. With practically every pack of cigarettes they opened, they warned me, "Don't ever start smoking." (Smoking is now so offensive to me that they needn't have worried.) The unspoken message I heard was, "I'm an adult, I can break my own rule, but *you* have to follow it." With reading, it's not "Don't do this," but rather the *absence* of something you've been doing as a child that many adults no longer do. When we tell our children to read, read, read, and they don't see *us* reading, that sends the message that reading is just one of those things you have to do as a kid. It's an activity you can give up when you're an adult. To such people, reading is really not important. If it were, adults would keep doing it.

A few years ago, I gave a presentation to a group of parents at a preschool learning center. I spoke about the importance of reading, discussing ways to get their kids interested in reading, how they can promote and encourage reading. One of the parents in the group raised her hand and said, "I understand what you're saying, but I really don't think reading is a big deal."

That stopped me in my tracks. I thought she was joking. "You mean you don't think reading is important?" I asked.

She shook her head. "No, not really. I've got a good job, I only read what I have to for work. I don't think it's that important."

I truly believe this woman wasn't trying to be confrontational or to get a rise out of me. She literally did not see the importance of reading in her life or the lives of her children, at least beyond the initial learning stage. I looked around the room at the rest of the parents and saw mostly indifference on their faces, *except* from the faces of several Latina women who looked like they were ready to declare war on this woman. (These Latina women had also been paying very close attention to my presentation, hanging on every word.)

This woman's opinion was one I had never encountered before and to be honest, I didn't know how to respond to her, other than to point out all the benefits that come from reading (better education, good job, etc.) which she could undoubtedly understand, and a love for reading (leading to a richer life), which she *couldn't* understand.

Because I work in a library where most of our patrons *do* recognize the importance of reading, I don't often encounter the type of indifferent attitude about reading presented by this parent, but those people are out there. Again, it's not that they *can't* read (although sometimes that is the case), but that they *don't*.

My library is very fortunate. We have a very high door count, very high circulation numbers, and very high attendance at library programs. We also have a large percentage of parents who *do* recognize the importance of reading and seek to develop a love of reading in their children. We don't see the types of parents I described above because the library holds no interest for them. They also don't realize libraries are about much more than just books. They normally think the library is the place you to go vote, and that's all[10]. You usually only meet people like the woman I described when you go outside the doors of the library.

I fear we will see more reactions like the one I experienced at that preschool learning center. I don't want my final chapter in this book to become a rant or a lament on the current state of reading in America, but I *am* concerned. When I discuss this problem with

---

10   Actually, that's not all. Lately you can add to that list people who come to the library *only* to pick up free Covid test kits and N95 masks.

others, I often hear blame directed at the internet. The internet is a tool, and like any other tool, it can be misused or overused. Even before we had the internet, the importance of reading still had its challenges and it probably always will. It's always been a struggle, but it's more of a struggle now than it once was, and I think I may know one of the reasons why.

As I mentioned before, reading is like a contract between the author and the reader. Readers must do their part, which includes thinking, processing, and meditating on what they've read, asking questions like, "Do I agree with what the author says? Disagree? Does the author make a valid point, even if it's in direct opposition to my own opinion? Is this other opinion worth thinking about? What would my life be like if I subscribed to this opinion? What would it look like to embrace this opinion or worldview?"

There are a multitude of other questions we as readers could ask ourselves when confronted with books that challenge us in various ways. But it's much easier *not* to read those books, especially if we already have our minds made up that *we're* right about certain issues, and others are wrong.

Don't we also see this in regular face-to-face conversations? We normally don't want to engage in discussions with people who don't share our opinions, at least beyond an initial encounter (unless we're spoiling for a fight). So many people have lost the ability to engage on a civil level with those who embrace opposing viewpoints, especially without descending to the level of anger and name-calling. Engaging with books presents the same problem, except we're engaging with an author on a page instead of a person in front of us. Since we can't rant against a book (Actually, you *can*, but people will just stare at you), we're forced to either put the book down, return it to the library (without taking your anger out on the book and damaging it) if it's not ours, or put it in the donations pile if it belongs to us. But the concepts that are challenging you are still in your mind. You must do something with them. You can take what you've read and disagree with it, ignore it, meditate on it, or embrace it, but you must do *something* with it. Maybe you'll discuss it with someone. Maybe you'll write a review of it. Maybe you'll write your own book. Maybe you'll realize, as I did (see Chapter 13), that you were wrong about something and owe someone an apology.

And just maybe you'll have an unexpected opportunity to plant a seed in someone's life, someone who, like the woman I described a few paragraphs back, doesn't see the need to read for pleasure. Maybe you'll encounter people from different circumstances in totally unexpected places. It happened to me.

Many years ago, when I had just started working at the library, I was at a local pizza takeout place waiting for my order. As is my usual practice, I had a book with me and was reading it. The book was so engrossing that I didn't realize there was a man talking to me. He was white, probably in his early 40s, his clothes a bit ragged and worn, but not dirty. I didn't think he was homeless, but maybe he was down on his luck. He said something about my reading a book while waiting for a pizza. I didn't know if he was simply commenting, trying to push my buttons, or what. I told him, "Yeah, I always carry a book. You never know when you might have some time to read."

I figured he was going to dismiss me or say something derogatory, but he sat down next to me in the waiting area. "You know," he said, "I'd never read a book in my life until last year."

This I wasn't expecting.

"Everybody I ran into," he continued, "was talking about *The Da Vinci Code*. That's all I heard about: *The Da Vinci Code, The Da Vinci Code*. I wanted to see what everyone was talking about, so I got a copy." (He didn't say where or how he got it.)

The man took a deep breath, let it out, and continued. "Man, I struggled to get through that book. All those names, all those words in other languages… But I kept at it, and I finally finished it. The first book I'd ever read." He looked proud of his accomplishment, and to tell the truth, I was proud of him, too.

I congratulated him and then asked, "So what do you want to read next?"

He froze for a moment, then shrugged. "I don't know. Something exciting, I guess."

A whole list of author suggestions ran through my mind, which I shared with him: Lee Child's Jack Reacher novels, something by Vince Flynn, or maybe a Harlan Coben thriller. We weren't far from the Crofton Library, so I told him he could go there and find books by those authors. Plus, the people at the Information Desk could help him find other authors and titles. The man looked down at the floor and frowned, and I realized he was either reluctant or embarrassed to ask for help. Maybe he didn't have a library card and felt uncomfortable applying for one. "They'll be glad to help you," I encouraged him.

"We'll see," he said. By this time his pizza was ready. He took it and walked away.

The next day I found a paperback copy of Harlan Coben's thriller *Gone for Good* (2002) at a thrift store and kept it in my car, hoping I would run into this guy again at the pizza place and could give the book to him.

I never saw him again. I hope he kept reading, is still reading, and is enjoying reading. What I want for that guy is what I want for everyone: to read, keep reading, and enjoy reading.

In her 2018 book *Reader, Come Home: The Reading Brain in a Digital World*, Maryanne Wolf quotes Marcel Proust, who wrote that "our own wisdom begins where that of the author leaves off, and would like him to provide answers, when all he can do is provide us with desires[11]." Those desires are often what's at the heart of reading for me, and I think also for the gentlemen in the Guys Book Club. Sure, sometimes we just want to read something light, fun, and entertaining, but sometimes we want answers, not simply an intake of information, but works that will challenge us as readers, force us to face hard questions, reexamine ideas and philosophies we once thought we held rigidly in place. Some might mistake such a desire as being unstable in our thinking or perhaps compromising our integrity or beliefs. Far from it. I want to see minds expanded, thoughts challenged. As far as reading, this can be attempted on a very high level or could manifest itself simply as a desire to better understand someone else's point of view. If someone asked me to tell them what the Guys Book Club is all about in three words, I'd reply:

Read. Discuss. Reflect.

I try my best to do those first two with the guys. The last one is up to them.

This book can't capture every memory, book, or discussion we've shared in the past ten years, but I hope it's given you, the reader, a taste of what the Guys Book Club is all about. As I mentioned in my

---

11 Poland, Warren S. "Reading Fiction and the Psychoanalytic Experience: Proust on Reading and on Reading Proust," 2003. https://pdfs.semanticscholar.org/aa80/ac84b b11318b144cbe4e5d803e39e7437eb4.pdf

discussion with Don in starting his own group, this isn't the only way to run a book club, but it's the one I'm comfortable with, and, apparently, the guys are comfortable with it as well.

The Guys Book Club has far exceeded the expectations I had for it all those years ago. That's largely due to a great group of men who love to read, discuss, and reflect on a wide variety of topics each month. They both challenge and inspire me. Thank you, gentlemen, for joining me on this adventure (which is still ongoing!).

If anyone reading this book would like more information about starting a book club for guys (of any age), I'd be more than happy to answer any questions you might have. Although it is mostly concerned with movies, you can reach me anytime at my website, https://www.andywolverton.com.

Keep reading, discussing, and reflecting.

The Pandemic and Beyond

finished writing most of this book well before the beginning of 2020, having said everything I'd wanted to say, but the pandemic obviously had other ideas. When our library system (and just about everything else in the world) shut down in March of 2020, I didn't know what was going to happen from one day to the next. None of us did. As we learned more about COVID-19, the Guys Book Club was on my mind primarily due to my concern of how the coronavirus would affect the more senior members of the group. I hoped and prayed everyone would be safe and well.

When it became obvious that the pandemic was going to last several months instead of a few weeks, I began hearing from some of the guys, asking when we would be able to meet again. I told them I had no idea, but it was good to communicate with them. I didn't even think about a virtual meeting of any kind until the head of the library's Virtual Services department contacted me, not about the Guys Book Club, but regarding my other library program, The Great Movies. In just a few days, we set up a virtual movie discussion via Zoom. Library headquarters wanted me to select movies from Kanopy, the library's streaming service, films that would be positive, uplifting, and hopeful. That's exactly what we did, and thanks to my wonderful cohost, Darnice Jasper, we made the program popular and successful. Then I thought, why not do this with the Guys Book Club?

I emailed the guys and told them that we were going to begin meeting, at least for the time being, virtually through Zoom. The pandemic had forced us to cancel our March 2020 discussion of *Grant* by Ron Chernow, a massive book everyone was eagerly looking forward to reading and discussing. Now we would be able to meet, at least virtually, and talk about the book. Our discussion was set for early April, and for a while it looked as if we'd found the way to make the best of a terrible situation. Not only did I very much want to meet with the guys, but I also wanted to reestablish some sense of normalcy in a chaotic, frightened world.

Only the reaction to the new format wasn't what I'd expected. Some of the guys were very reluctant to meet virtually. A few weren't comfortable with the technology, never having used Zoom before. Others were okay with Zoom, but didn't necessarily like it. Three of the members emailed me to say that while they appreciated the effort I was making to meet virtually, they would not be joining us, preferring instead to wait until we could meet in person.

I felt that most of the group would attend virtually, but I had another problem: how to get books into their hands. I had already chosen the next several titles for the in-person group, but there was no way for the guys to get them: Libraries were closed and book drops were locked, so no books were going out or coming in. Since most members of the group had already read *Grant* (or still had it checked out), that book wasn't going to be a problem, but we couldn't discuss the other scheduled books since no one could access the library copies. So *now* what?

I'd always wanted to discuss more classics in the group, and this seemed the perfect time to start. I found several titles that we had practically unlimited copies of in the form of downloadable eBooks or audiobooks. Even if the titles *were* limited, I found links to free versions of most of the books.

To make this transition as painless as possible, the first book needed to be both short and familiar. I figured that everyone in the group had probably read my first pick, Robert Louis Stevenson's *The Strange Case of Dr. Jekyll and Mr. Hyde,* but such was not the case. Although some of the guys had read the slim novel (actually a novella) in school, memories of the several movie adaptations filled their minds. Yet they were all struck with how effective Stevenson's story remains for modern readers, recognizing that we all, despite our best efforts to contain him, have a little bit of Mr. Hyde in us.

Our June title, Daniel Defoe's *Robinson Crusoe,* surprised me in that most of the men had never read it before, but they enjoyed it. Some mentioned that the book reminded them of the Tom Hanks movie *Cast Away* (2000), and most confessed that *Robinson Crusoe* far exceeded their expectations. The group seemed more comfortable with this second virtual discussion, so maybe these Zoom meetings were going to bring in more guys.

My next pick was risky, and I knew it. For years I'd had the idea of discussing a book of poetry, but our system doesn't have that many books of modern poetry, and when it does, there usually aren't enough copies for a group our size. I also personally wanted to read T. S. Eliot's *The Waste Land,* so I chose that for our July discussion. Of course, I had never read *The Waste Land*...

After a few pages I thought, "Oh boy. This is gonna be tough." After reading the poem and doing some fairly serious research on it, I began to regret my choice. I certainly didn't understand most of what was going on after my initial reading, so I studied it more. Soon the amount of writing and scholarship on the poem grew overwhelming. Knowing that one of our employees, Jenna Novosel, had just finished a degree in English, I asked her if she was familiar with the work. Jenna said that she was and shared some of her research with me. This crash course in *The Waste Land* certainly helped, but there was no way I would be able to digest all of this research in time for the program. I asked Jenna to join us as a special guest to give us insight into the poem, which she did. Eliot's masterwork was a struggle for many of us (including me), but I believe we were all the richer for it.

You have to be careful with assumptions. I assumed that many of the guys had read Jack London's *The Call of the Wild* in their younger days, but most (once again, including me) hadn't. Although we were all startled at the brutality of a book that appears on many reading lists for middle school (or younger) kids, no one disputed the novel's brilliance or London's gift for storytelling.

In time the library began offering curbside service, which meant patrons could place holds on books and have staff bring them out to a table in the front of the library. (*Technically* not curbside service, but not too many people seemed to complain.) I began choosing some of the books we had previously voted for, such as *All the Light We Cannot See* by Anthony Doerr, *Say Nothing: A True Story of Murder and Memory in Northern Ireland* by Patrick Radden Keefe, and our 100th book, appropriately titled *The Library Book* by Susan Orlean.

During our virtual meetings, several interesting things happened. We began to have participants from other parts of the country. A man in Florida had a Maryland relative who told him about the book club, so he signed up online. Two librarians in Dade County, Florida joined us for our discussion of Frank Herbert's science fiction classic *Dune* (led by my coworker Colin Chappel), since they were putting together their own Dune book club in anticipation of the 2020 movie (delayed until December 2021). Others joined from time to time, some of them from right here in Anne Arundel County.

Then a very interesting thing happened. The regular members who said they would never be a part of the virtual club came back. They didn't make a big deal about it, and neither did I, but I can't tell you how delighted I was to have them joining us again.

As I write this in September 2021, we are still meeting virtually. Many library programs are still virtual, and so are we, at least for a few more weeks. However, I am planning an in-person celebration of the group's 10th anniversary in October 2021.

What does the future hold, not only for this book club, but *any* book club? Or for reading? How did the pandemic change our reading habits? Did many non-readers pick up a book or two during the lockdown?

I heard many comments from our curbside patrons and even more when appointments began: "Thank you for curbside! Before that, I kept reading the same books over and over," and "Now I can stop buying new books online," and the most frequent (and heartwarming) comment, "Thank God for the library! I couldn't have made it through all this without you!"

This was all fine, but it still wasn't normal. I missed relationships with patrons, the readers' advisory with some of our regulars (particularly the guy who will read most any work of crime fiction I recommend), the discussions of "What should I read next?" or even the "Nice seeing you" farewells on their way out the door. Even more, I missed the sense of community I had with the book group.

I realized this when I joined a different online book discussion that had nothing to do with the library. I knew a few of the people in the group, but some of them I'd only seen virtually. During those Zoom meetings, one guy seemed quiet, reserved, and very serious. Maybe beyond serious. He didn't smile much and seemed a little intimidating. I thought he might be difficult to get to know, maybe even impossible during virtual meetings.

Then after restrictions began to relax and things opened up, the group began to meet in person. This same person attended, and I was astounded to discover that he was shorter than me (and I'm of average height), totally relaxed, frequently laughed along with us, and contributed positively to the group. People - or at least some people - act differently in a virtual setting. Interacting with them in person can be a completely different experience.

I realized from participating in this other group that perhaps many of us were not entirely ourselves virtually. Even if we were, everyone has different computer equipment, different internet speeds, at-home distractions, and many other things that you don't have to worry about during in-person meetings. Even after several months of virtual book discussions, the comfort level was increasing, but members of the Guys Book Club (including me) still weren't *ourselves*. When the pandemic began I'd spent nine years with these guys meeting in the same room month after month. And then we were meeting on computers, tablets, smart phones, sometimes with connectivity issues, sometimes with noises in the background. (There's always someone who forgets to mute themselves when they're not talking. Sometimes it's me.)

A book club is a place where people can get together and discuss books. Part of the fun of such meetings is to hear the excitement in someone's voice as they comment on a book, the enthusiasm that can't be hidden from their eyes. (It's also there when they *don't* like a certain book.) You can't fully see someone's body language, facial expressions, or attentiveness when you're online. The sharing of opinions, comments, questions, and information just isn't the same virtually as it is when we're all in the same room.

Plus, I know that certain comments will initiate responses from certain members. Our group consists of medical professionals, educators, writers, former military, and people from many other walks of life. I know that when comments relevant to those professions come up, the people who've been there will have valuable insights to share. If you're meeting in person, you can watch those moments develop, the same way you can watch a good sports team work together. A good discussion often develops that way, and it's a thing of beauty to see it unfold. This is impossible during a virtual program.

At my local church yesterday, the congregation sang indoors without masks for the first time in over a year. It was like hearing music for the first time. The sound wasn't filtered, muffled, or restricted in any way. I feared that after months of singing into dense material that people would forget how to sing. Instead it was strong, powerful, almost overwhelming. You could hear the joy as it passed through each person's lips, blending into a thing of true beauty. It literally brought me to tears.

The first in-person meeting of the Guys Book Club certainly won't be the same experience as I had in church. But it will be just as joyous, just as liberating. We'll talk, laugh, share, maybe disagree about the books we're reading. But we'll do it together, in the same room.

One of the lessons the pandemic taught me (and hopefully others) is that people need to be together. It's how we communicate, work, play, solve problems, laugh, cry. It's how we build community. There's a reason that misunderstandings frequently happen over texts, email, letters (remember those?), and even phone conversations. None of those methods of communication carry the same potency as an in-person face-to-face discussion. Sure, those interactions can be vague and opaque as well, but there's at least a good opportunity for clarity and understanding.

I long for this. I think the guys do, too.

As of this writing, the group is scheduled to meet in-person in October 2021, our first face-to-face meeting in 18 months. I've thought about what book we'll discuss, if we'll talk about what other books we read during the pandemic, or books we want to read next. We may not talk about books at all, but simply catch up. I've also thought about just getting together to share stories of the group's past ten years, since October will mark our 10th anniversary.

It really doesn't matter what we talk about. The community has been built, and the community needs to come together again. It may be awkward at first, but we'll get the hang of it. We'll move forward. We'll keep reading and discussing.

"All the things that are wrong in the world seem conquered by a library's simple unspoken promise: Here I am, please tell me your story; here is my story, please listen."

—Susan Orlean, *The Library Book*

"You think your pain and your heartbreak are unprecedented in the history of the world, but then you read. It was books that taught me that the things that tormented me most were the very things that connected me with all the people who were alive, who had ever been alive."

—James Baldwin

"Friendship is born at that moment when one person says to another: "What! You too? I thought I was the only one."

—C.S. Lewis, *The Four Loves*

ACKNOWLEDGMENTS

Looking back over the past ten years, I have many people to thank for the success of the Guys Book Club. First, my former supervisor Heather Leonard, who listened to and approved my crazy idea. Second, my former branch manager Karen Mansbridge, who gave me the green light for getting the group off the ground and provided a wealth of wisdom for keeping it going.

My coworker Samantha Zline has given me invaluable advice through the years and has helped me with advertising and marketing.

My current supervisor Nisa Popper has provided a never-ending source of encouragement, providing valuable wisdom and direction. Nisa has also been a constant rock of strength during the troubled and uncertain times of the pandemic.

Thanks to all my coworkers who frequently promote the book club to those who come up to the Info Desk and answer their inquiries.

Phil Ferrara (who for many years has run his own book club for guys, independent of the library) has provided me with a wealth of information and advice through the years and always asks how the group is doing. Thank you, Phil.

Many thanks to Steve Collier, for his excellent introduction.

Paul Stillwell and Jim Haas, both excellent writers, read earlier drafts of the book and have not only given me expert advice and guidance, but are also wonderful friends. Thank you, gentlemen.

Thanks to Cathy Hollerbach, who also read the book and gave me excellent comments and support.

My wife Cindy read and proofread this manuscript, but, more importantly, kept at me to persevere with the project, which saw many stops and starts. She is always there with love and encouragement.

Finally, a big thank you to all the guys who have been and continue to be part of the Guys Book Club at the Severna Park Library. Let's keep this thing going. Never stop reading, discussing, and reflecting.

GUYS BOOK CLUB READING LIST
SEVERNA PARK LIBRARY

2011

October – *Unbroken: A World War II Story of Survival, Resilience, and Redemption* – Laura Hillenbrand

November – *Born to Run: A Hidden Tribe, Superathletes, and the Greatest Race the World Has Never Seen* – Christopher McDougall

2012

January – *The Maltese Falcon* – Dashiell Hammett

March – *Moneyball: The Art of Winning an Unfair Game* – Michael Lewis

May – *No Country for Old Men* – Cormac McCarthy

August – *Destiny of the Republic: A Tale of Madness, Medicine, and the Murder of a President* – Candice Millard

September – *In Defense of Food: An Eater's Manifesto* – Michael Pollan

October – *Outliers: The Story of Success* – Malcolm Gladwell

November – *A Walk in the Woods: Rediscovering America on the Appalachian Trail* – Bill Bryson

December – *True Grit* – Charles Portis

2013

January – *Good to Great: Why Some Companies Make the Leap... and Others Don't* – Jim Collins

February – *Outcasts United: An American Town, a Refugee Team, and One Woman's Quest to Make a Difference* – Warren St. John

March – *The Sun also Rises* – Ernest Hemingway

April – *Hellhound on His Trail: The Stalking of Martin Luther King, Jr. and the International Hunt for His Assassin* – Hampton Sides

May – *Quiet: The Power of Introverts in a World That Can't Stop Talking* – Susan Cain

June – *Maus I: A Survivor's Tale* – Art Spiegelman

July – *The Great Gatsby* – F. Scott Fitzgerald

August – *Enemies: A History of the FBI* – Tim Weiner

September – *The Killer Angels* – Michael Shaara

October – *The Fall of the House of Usher and Other Writings* – Edgar Allan Poe

November – *Team of Rivals: The Political Genius of Abraham Lincoln* – Doris Kearns Goodwin

December – *City of Thieves* – David Benioff

2014

January – *Hatchet* – Gary Paulsen

February – *My Losing Season: A Memoir* – Pat Conroy

March – *The Doorbell Rang* – Rex Stout

April – *The Brilliant Disaster: JFK, Castro, and American's Doomed Invasion of Cuba's Bay of Pigs* – Jim Rasenberger

May – *Superman: The High-Flying History of America's Most Enduring Hero* – Larry Tye

June – *Motherless Brooklyn* – Jonathan Lethem

July – *The Guns of August* – Barbara W. Tuchman

August – *The Generals: American Military Command from World War II to Today* – Thomas E. Ricks

September – *The Goldfinch* – Donna Tartt

October – *A Good Man is Hard to Find and Other Stories* – Flannery O'Connor

November – *The River of Doubt: Theodore Roosevelt's Darkest Journey* – Candice Millard

December – *Slaughterhouse-Five* – Kurt Vonnegut

2015

January – *Flash Boys: A Wall Street Revolt* – Michael Lewis

February – *Power, Faith and Fantasy: America in the Middle East 1776 to the Present* – Michael B. Oren

March – *Code Word Paternity: A Presidential Thriller* – Doug Norton

April – *The Brothers: John Foster Dulles, Allen Dulles, and Their Secret World War* – Stephen Kinzer

May – *The Right Stuff* – Tom Wolfe

June – *The Good Spy: The Life and Death of Robert Ames* – Kai Bird

July – *Operation Mincemeat: How a Dead Man and a Bizarre Plan Fooled the Nazis and Assured an Allied Victory* – Ben Macintyre

August – *The Perfect Storm* – Sebastian Junger

September – *The Princess Bride* – William Goldman

October – *In Cold Blood* – Truman Capote

November – *The Golden Thirteen: Recollections of the First Black Naval Officers* – Paul Stillwell

December – *The Cellist of Sarajevo* – Steven Galloway

2016

January – *Pride and Prejudice* – Jane Austen

February – *Orphan Train* – Christina Baker Kline

March – *The Wright Brothers* – David McCullough

April – *The Boys in the Boat* – Daniel James Brown

May – *Operation Nemesis: The Assassination Plot that Avenged the Armenian Genocide* – Eric Bogosian

June – *Undaunted Courage: Meriwether Lewis, Thomas Jefferson, and the Opening of the American West* – Stephen E. Ambrose

July – *The Finest Hours: The True Story of the U.S. Coast Guard's Most Daring Sea Rescue* – Michael J. Tougias, Casey Sherman

August – *Midnight in the Garden of Good and Evil* – John Berendt

September – *The Nightingale* – Kristin Hannah

October – Eisenhower in War and Peace – Jean Edward Smith

November – *The Mathews Men: Seven Brothers and the War Against Hitler's U-Boats* – William Geroux

December – *A Spy Among Friends: Kim Philby and the Great Betrayal* – Ben Macintyre

2017

January – *Black Flags: The Rise of ISIS* – Joby Warrick

February – *Hero of the Empire: The Boer War, a Daring Escape, and the Making of Winston Churchill* – Candice Millard

CONTENTS

2018

September – *Sapiens: A Brief History of Humankind* – Yuval Noah Harari

October – *Bloodsworth: The True Story of the First Death Row Inmate Exonerated by DNA* – Tim Junkin

November – *Warlight* – Michael Ondaatje

December – *The Lost City of the Monkey God* – Douglas Preston

2019

January – *Lost in Math: How Beauty Leads Physics Astray* – Sabine Hossenfelder

February – *Kindred* – Octavia E. Butler

March – *I'll Be Gone in the Dark: One Woman's Obsessive Search for the Golden State Killer* – Michelle McNamara

April – *Reader, Come Home: The Reading Brain in the Digital World* – Maryanne Wolf

May – *Why We Sleep: Unlocking the Power of Sleep and Dreams* – Matthew Walker

June – *The Immortalists* – Chloe Benjamin

July – *The First Conspiracy: The Secret Plot to Kill George Washington* – Brad Meltzer, Josh Mensch

August – *Leadership in Turbulent Times* – Doris Kearns Goodwin

September – *The Guernsey Literary and Potato Peel Pie Society* – Mary Ann Shaffer

October – *Atomic Habits: An Easy & Proven Way to Build Good Habits & Break Bad Ones* – James Clear

November – *Over the Edge of the World: Magellan's Terrifying Circumnavigation of the Globe* – Laurence Bergreen

CONTENTS

April – *First Principles: What America's Founders Learned from the Greeks and Romans and How That Shaped Our Country* – Thomas E. Ricks (virtual)

May – *I Got a Monster: The Rise and Fall of America's Most Corrupt Police Squad* – Baynard Woods, Brandon Soderberg (virtual)

June – *Something Wicked This Way Comes* – Ray Bradbury (virtual)

July – *Secondhand Time: The Last of the Soviets* – Svetlana Alexievich (virtual)

August – *The Warmth of Other Suns* – Isabel Wilkerson (virtual)

September – *Just Mercy: A Story of Justice and Redemption* – Bryan Stevenson (virtual)

October - 10th Anniversary Celebration (in-person meetings resume)

November - *Still Life* - Louise Penny

December - *Deacon King Kong* - James McBride

2022

January - meeting postponed

February - *Stranger in the Woods: The Extraordinary Story of the Last True Hermit* - Michael Finkel

ABOUT THE AUTHOR

Andy Wolverton is a librarian at the Severna Park Library in Severna Park, Maryland, part of the Anne Arundel County Public Library system. He leads the Guys Book Club and The Great Movies, a monthly series in which he introduces, screens, and leads discussions of classic films. You can find his other writings in *The Dark Pages: The Newsletter for Film Noir Lovers*, and at his website, www.andywolverton.com.